# Cambridge Elements

Elements in Philosophy and Logic
edited by
Bradley Armour-Garb
*SUNY Albany*
Frederick Kroon
*The University of Auckland*

# LOGICAL PLURALISM

Colin R. Caret
*Utrecht University*

Shaftesbury Road, Cambridge CB2 8EA, United Kingdom

One Liberty Plaza, 20th Floor, New York, NY 10006, USA

477 Williamstown Road, Port Melbourne, VIC 3207, Australia

314–321, 3rd Floor, Plot 3, Splendor Forum, Jasola District Centre,
New Delhi – 110025, India

103 Penang Road, #05–06/07, Visioncrest Commercial, Singapore 238467

Cambridge University Press is part of Cambridge University Press & Assessment,
a department of the University of Cambridge.

We share the University's mission to contribute to society through the pursuit of
education, learning and research at the highest international levels of excellence.

www.cambridge.org
Information on this title: www.cambridge.org/9781009478557

DOI: 10.1017/9781009189583

© Colin R. Caret 2025

This publication is in copyright. Subject to statutory exception and to the provisions
of relevant collective licensing agreements, no reproduction of any part may take
place without the written permission of Cambridge University Press & Assessment.

When citing this work, please include a reference to the DOI 10.1017/9781009189583

First published 2025

*A catalogue record for this publication is available from the British Library*

ISBN 978-1-009-47855-7 Hardback
ISBN 978-1-009-18957-6 Paperback
ISSN 2516-418X (online)
ISSN 2516-4171 (print)

Cambridge University Press & Assessment has no responsibility for the persistence
or accuracy of URLs for external or third-party internet websites referred to in this
publication and does not guarantee that any content on such websites is, or will
remain, accurate or appropriate.

For EU product safety concerns, contact us at Calle de José Abascal, 56, 1°, 28003
Madrid, Spain, or email eugpsr@cambridge.org

# Logical Pluralism

Elements in Philosophy and Logic

DOI: 10.1017/9781009189583
First published online: September 2025

---

Colin R. Caret
*Utrecht University*

**Author for correspondence:** Colin R. Caret, colin.caret@protonmail.com

**Abstract:** Logical pluralism is the view that there is more than one correct logic. This view emerged in a dialectical context in which certain laws of logic were hotly debated by philosophers. For example, philosophers have spilled a great deal of ink over the logical principle of explosion ("from a contradiction, everything follows"). One side in the debate accepts this principle, the other side rejects it. It is exceedingly natural to assume that these rival points of view are incompatible, hence one side of the debate is correct while the other is incorrect. This is logical monism: the view that there is exactly one correct logic. Pluralists argue that the monistic assumption is subtly and surprisingly wrong. According to the pluralist, some logics that appear to be irreconcilable rivals are, in fact, both correct in their own ways. This Element will explain the debate over logical pluralism in an accessible manner.

**Keywords:** logical consequence, truth, meaning, normativity, pluralism

© Colin R. Caret 2025

ISBNs: 9781009478557 (HB), 9781009189576 (PB), 9781009189583 (OC)
ISSNs: 2516-418X (online), 2516-4171 (print)

# Contents

| | | |
|---|---|---:|
| | Introduction | 1 |
| 1 | Doing Logic | 3 |
| 2 | Pluralistic Perspectives | 30 |
| 3 | Challenges | 59 |
| | Final Thoughts | 75 |
| | References | 77 |

## Introduction

Logical pluralism is the view that there is more than one correct logic. A logic is a formal system that gives an account of valid arguments or proofs. There are many *interesting* logics, to be sure, but we might expect just one of them to be *correct* at the end of the day. Pluralism upends this expectation with its endorsement of many logics.

Ideally, a pluralist view will offer us a satisfying path between unity and plurality. On the one hand, the pluralist should draw a meaningful distinction between *logic* and *other* subject matters. Doing so bestows a significant unity to the phenomenon. It tells us how we know that we are talking about different instances of one and the same thing. On the other hand, this distinction should be drawn in a way that allows more than one thing to be correctly categorized on the side of logic. It is a useful exercise to reflect on which versions of logical pluralism successfully navigate this path.

There are a number of well-known sources of diversity and uncertainty in logic that do not rise to the level of pluralism. For one thing, the field of logic is largely unified by its tools. Modern logicians heavily rely on mathematical systems called *formal logics* and these systems are quite flexible. Formal logics are widely used in technical applications such as circuit design and computer program verification, but these applications are somewhat orthogonal to the traditional philosophical aims of logic. It is completely uncontroversial to say that there is more than one useful formal logic for technical applications. This is not open to debate and it is not what logical pluralists care about.

When philosophers discuss the subject matter of logic, they often use value terms like "good reasoning" and "rationality," but these normative concepts raise all sorts of challenges for philosophy and logic. An agent who prefers efficient solutions to problems might value different methods of reasoning than an agent who prefers more accurate solutions. Both types of reasoning are good in their own way. An expressivist about normative appraisals might even say that statements about good reasoning and rational belief do not have determinate content. If logic is entwined with these issues, it may be impossible for us to *justify* one logic over another. Still, diffuse skepticism about rationality and the justification of logic are also not what logical pluralists care about.

Logical pluralism stakes out a different position altogether. It says that there is a many-one relationship between logics *qua* formal theories, and the phenomena that these theories are intended to study or codify. We cannot isolate one logic that triumphs over all others. Pluralists have a number of different reasons for holding this view.

Some pluralists consider logics to either be creative devices or at best only indirectly conducive to an understanding of their target phenomena. On this type of view, logics play an active role in regimenting the concept of validity and more than one logic successfully fulfills this task. Another strand of pluralism contends that our preexisting concept of validity is underspecified in a distinctive way. On this type of view, logics target an interesting property, but we discover that this really bifurcates into more than one property of the same kind. Pluralists claim, for various reasons, that it is futile to search for a single, uniquely correct logic. More than one logic satisfies the criteria we care about and there is "no further fact of the matter" about which logic is correct (Restall, 2002, p. 426).

Obviously, there is much more to say about this research program. What is validity, how do we theorize this phenomenon, and why do these factors allegedly conspire to produce pluralism? Does pluralism imply that all logics are equal? When logicians disagree about the correct logic, does logical pluralism imply that these logicians are talking past one other or stuck in a pointless muddle? Is logical pluralism a stable and coherent view in the first place? Does it have any interesting consequences for how we think about the foundations of science and mathematics? This Element addresses such issues.

The earliest seeds of logical pluralism are found in the work of Alfred Tarski and Rudolph Carnap from the 1930s onward. It is unclear whether they would have accepted modern versions of the view, but their ideas were a great source of inspiration for logical pluralists. Susan Haack first used the term "logical pluralism" in roughly the modern sense, relating it to several other points of view on logical systems. Haack tentatively defends logical pluralism by drawing on ideas about scientific model-building.

The current debate on logical pluralism kicked off in the early 2000s with the ambitious work of Jc Beall and Greg Restall. They advanced an interesting pluralist view of logic that sparked dozens of responses from both critical and sympathetic points of view. It is fair to say that the vast majority of the recent literature on pluralism is connected to this particular theory in some way; but as the literature matured, it also extended well beyond the idiosyncrasies of Beall and Restall's view. Another excellent inroad to this debate is the Stanford Encyclopedia's entry "Logical Pluralism" (Russell, 2021).

Logical pluralism has its detractors. There is some pushback from the perspective of the history of logic, while other problems are alleged to be internal to the pluralist view itself. As we will see, there are quite a few versions of logical pluralism. It often seems as if different pluralists advocate for views quite unrelated to one another. My greatest hope for this Element is that it tells a convincing story about the natural evolution of pluralist thought from its early roots to its current state.

This Element is written in the hope that it will be accessible to a wide swath of readers. It does not rely on extensive prior knowledge. To that end, the Element has three parts. Section 1 offers a mini-textbook treatment of the modern practices of formal logic. This clarifies the sort of thing that philosophers are concerned with when they raise questions about correct logic(s). Section 2 covers the history of logical pluralism, different approaches to pluralism, as well as some discussion of how these views contrast with each other. Section 3 reviews some of the prominent worries that have been lodged against logical pluralism and how pluralists may handle these worries.

# 1 Doing Logic

## 1.1 Validity

Logic is concerned with good arguments and, most especially, with *proofs* (arguments that are important in mathematics and abstract theory-building). It is good for arguments to be clear and economical, but logic is not concerned with those stylistic features. Logic is concerned with a standard of *correctness* for arguments, known as *validity*.

Here is a typical example of a valid argument.

---

**Example 1**

(1.1) All dogs are mammals.
(1.2) All mammals are animals.
∴ All dogs are animals.

---

This argument starts with premises (1.1) and (1.2) and ends with the concluding sentence "All dogs are animals." The conclusion is marked with the special symbol "∴." We can read this symbol as expressing the phrase "Therefore...." To check whether this argument is valid we need to *evaluate* the connection between its premises and conclusion.

When we say that an argument is valid (correct), it means that the right kind of connection is really there; if the connection is missing, the argument is invalid (incorrect). Standard textbook logic says that Example 1 is valid; the premises of the argument really do support its conclusion; the conclusion follows from the premises. These are three different ways of expressing that the argument has the right logical properties.

The roots of this field of study in Western philosophy trace back to Aristotle: "A deduction is speech (logos) in which, certain things having been supposed, something different from those supposed results of necessity because of their being so" (*Prior Analytics* I.2, 24b18–20, trans. Smith 1989).

The translation of this passage uses the word "deduction" to refer to roughly the same thing as a valid argument. Aristotle suggests that when we make certain assumptions, lo and behold, something else results *of necessity*. A deduction or valid argument expresses this kind of airtight connection between its premises and conclusion.

Good arguments and reasonable conclusions are just as important in empirical science as they are in logic. However, there is a difference in emphasis. Science is much more concerned with actual, observable facts. For example, a physicist might ask: Is it actually true that dark matter is composed of axion particles? This is a question about how things work in the physical world. Reasoning and argument are indirectly involved only because they can help scientists find good answers to their questions.

Logic directly concerns itself with reasoning and argument themselves. We can see logical questions as *hypotheticals*. A typical question of logic is something like this: assuming that everything in the universe is composed of axion particles, does it follow that dark matter is composed of axion particles? We do not need to know real physics to answer this question. It is not a question about matter or particles. The logical question is about *what follows from what*. Hypothetical thinking along these lines has an important role in all walks of life, but logic makes this into its primary topic of study.

If the conclusion of an argument really does follow from the premises by an airtight, necessary connection, then the argument is valid.

**Concept. (Valid Argument)** An argument whose conclusion follows from its premises.

It would be nice to know which arguments are valid. In modern logic, we build systematic accounts of validity. There are different accounts, hence different logics.

The main job of logic is to classify valid arguments. Logical pluralism says that there is more than one correct way to do this. In order to discuss this philosophical view, it might help to know something about the methods of modern logic.

The rest of this section introduces the methods of modern, formal logic. The goal is to showcase how minor variations and choices in these methods produce a variety of different logical systems. This will make certain aspects of logical pluralism much clearer. If you already know the difference between first-order logic and second-order logic, or that between classical logic and non-classical logic, you can skip ahead to the summary of key results in Section 1.5. For everyone else: read on.

## 1.2 Forms, Rules, Models

Perhaps the most important idea in modern logic is this: Validity is often determined by the internal structure or *logical form* of arguments. Some examples should help to make the idea of logical form clearer. Here is an example of an argument.

---
**Example 2**

(2.1) Fish swim.
(2.2) Birds fly.
∴ Fish swim and birds fly.

---

Here is another argument with the same form.

---
**Example 3**

(3.1) Water is wet.
(3.2) Fire is hot.
∴ Water is wet and fire is hot.

---

When we say that Examples 2 and 3 have the same form, what are we talking about? It probably seems quite obvious, but let's spell it out. Each argument has two premises. The conclusion is a more complex sentence that joins the premise sentences together with the word "and" between them. That pattern is exactly the same between both arguments. Formal logic uses such patterns to analyze which arguments are valid.

We use *formal languages* to make this sort of analysis clear. A formal language represents sentence parts with symbols. In this Element, we will use the lowercase letters $p, q, r$ to stand for whole, declarative sentences. We also have special *logical* symbols:

- The negation connective ¬ is read as the English word "not."
- The conjunction connective ∧ is read as the English word "and."
- The disjunction connective ∨ is read as the English word "or."
- The conditional connective → is read as the English phrase "if..., then...."

The rules for putting these symbols together create *formulas*. Each formula represents an underlying structure that occurs in many sentences, based on the parts of the sentence and how those parts are put together. An argument form is simply the collection of formulas that represent the logical forms of the sentences in the argument.

For example, here is the argument form shared by Examples 2 and 3.

**Example 4**

(4.1) $p$
(4.2) $q$
 $\therefore p \wedge q$

This should be easy enough to understand. The formula $p \wedge q$ represents a sentence in which the simpler sentence $p$ is joined with $q$ by putting the word "and" between them, just like we saw in Examples 2 and 3.

The type of logic that draws on this formal language is called *propositional* logic. It only focuses on the aspects of argument form that involve the placement of whole, declarative sentences and the logical connectives. We could imagine various ways to expand this formal language to represent other operators on sentences. For example, we could include symbols for *modalities.* In the formal language of modal logic, $\Box p$ says "$p$ is necessary" and $\Diamond p$ says "$p$ is possible." This allows us to represent a wider range of argument forms than is possible with just the basic language of propositional logic.

Here is another pair of examples to think about.

**Example 5**

(5.1) Alytus is small.
(5.2) Vilnius is large.
 $\therefore$ Something is small and something is large.

The following argument has the same form as the preceding one.

**Example 6**

(6.1) Chocolate is delicious.
(6.2) Vegemite is disgusting.
 $\therefore$ Something is delicious and something is disgusting.

When we say that Examples 5 and 6 have the same form, what are we talking about? Each argument has two premises that ascribe a property to some specific, named object. The conclusion sentence has the word "and" in the middle.

Each half of the conclusion sentence talks about one of the same properties from the premises, but instead of ascribing that property to a specific, named object, it says more generically that *something* has the salient property. Again, this pattern is exactly the same between both arguments.

To represent this kind of pattern we need a formal language that can represent the internal parts of sentences. We use the lowercase letters $a, b, c$ to stand for names of specific people, places, or things. We use the uppercase letters $F, G, H$ to stand for predicates, which express properties of things. We also need more *logical* symbols:

- The existential quantifier $\exists$ is read as the English phrase "there is...."
- The universal quantifier $\forall$ is read as the English phrase "for all...."
- The variables $x, y, z$ make clear how the quantifiers are used.

Here is the argument form shared by Examples 5 and 6.

---

**Example 7**

(7.1) $Fa$

(7.2) $Gc$

∴ $(\exists x Fx \land \exists y Gy)$

---

We read this as follows. $Fa$ represents the form of a sentence that applies predicate $F$ to name $a$, so it ascribes a property to some specific, named object. Likewise for $Gc$. This is just like the premises in Examples 5 and 6. $\exists x Fx$ attaches the quantifier phrase to a variable, which you can think about as a sort of "test" to see whether any chosen object has property $F$. In other words, $\exists x Fx$ represents the form of a sentence that says there is at least one thing that satisfies the $Fx$ "test," or in more natural English, it just says *something has property F*. Likewise, $\exists y Gy$ says that *something has property G*.

The type of logic that draws on this formal language is called *first-order* logic. It focuses not only on sentences and logical connectives, but other aspects of argument form that involve the placement of names, predicates, and objectual quantifiers. We could imagine various ways to expand this formal language to represent other types of quantifiers. For example, we could add *second-order* quantifiers to generalize over predicate position. In the language of second-order logic, $\forall X Xa$ says "All properties apply to $a$" and $\exists X Xc$ says "Some property applies to $c$." This allows us to represent a wider range of argument forms than is possible with just the basic language of first-order logic.

Formal languages draw our attention to specific aspects of sentence structure, which is extremely helpful for logical analysis, but it also involves a choice. Should our logical tools pay attention to modal operators or second-order quantifiers? These are not part of standard, introductory logic books.

Are modal operators or second-order quantifiers inappropriate for logical study? We will revisit this question about the *logical vocabulary* in Section 2.2 and consider whether it may be connected with logical pluralism.

Creating a formal language is only the first step into formal logic. The next natural question is: What do we do with this structural information? How can we use argument forms to classify valid arguments? There are two prominent techniques for doing this. One of them uses *proof rules*, the other uses *semantic models*.

Outside of formal logic, a proof is just a piece of conclusive reasoning. Most of us encounter proofs in mathematics. Just think about examples you have seen, like the proof that $\sqrt{2}$ is irrational or the proof of the Pythagorean theorem which states that $a^2 + b^2 = c^2$ for the edges of a right triangle. You may recall that these proofs involve a lot of steps. This is a key idea in *proof theory*, an important method for classifying valid arguments.

A formal analysis of proofs, also known as a *derivation*, is built up from individual steps. Each step involves a transition from input formulas to output formulas. The essence of proof theory is given by *proof rules* that tell us what steps are allowed. In some sense, our goal is to choose rules that are so secure that we can blindly follow them without ever making a mistake. The derivable arguments are all valid.

There is a second important technique for working with argument forms. Recall how Aristotle said that the conclusion of a valid argument results *of necessity*. This may suggest the idea that validity comes from an external relationship between sentences and the circumstances that make sentences true. A semantic model is a kind of precise representation or a mathematical abstraction of such a circumstance. This is the key idea in *model theory*, which is yet another method for classifying valid arguments.

In broad outline, models assign truth-values to formulas. A formula might be true in some models and not in others. We think of each model as a *logically possible* circumstance. Now, we can look for relationships between arguments and models. If every model that makes the premises true also makes the conclusion true, we say that such an argument is truth-preserving. The truth-preserving arguments are all valid.

In the next few sections, we will look at some details of proof theory and model theory to understand how these techniques are used to define different logics. Before moving on, there are a few more useful preliminary remarks to make.

In principle, we can take *any* formulas $p_1, p_2, \ldots$ and *any* single formula $q$ and think of them, respectively, as the premises and conclusion of an argument. This determines a class of argument forms. A specific formal technique divides that class into two parts: The valid arguments and the invalid arguments. Simply put, the result of using proof theory or model theory is to produce a demarcation of the set of valid argument forms. This is what we call an *extensional definition* of validity. It sometimes happens that we can use two different techniques to get exactly the same extensional definition. One of the most famous mathematical results in logic is called the Completeness Theorem, which basically shows that a proof theory and a model theory are extensionally equivalent.

In the next section, we will compare some famous formal logics known as classical, intuitionistic, and relevant logics. These "named logics" are not identified with just one specific proof theory or one specific model theory. When we talk about a logical system by name, what matters is the extensional definition of validity that goes along with that type of logic. There are different ways of doing proof theory or model theory that produce exactly the same logic in the extensional sense. When we find two different tools that define the same logic, like in the Completeness Theorem, then we have at least two ways of understanding the nature of that single notion of validity.

Logics are used to analyze arguments in the first place, but they also have repercussions for how we think about theories. A theory is a bunch of sentences, so we can think about what would happen if we treated those sentences as the premises of an argument. If conclusion $C$ follows from a theory, we say that $C$ is one of the *commitments* of that theory. These commitments are part of the implicit worldview of the theory. A theory can only be true if all of its commitments are true.

Adding information to a theory often causes its commitments to expand. If we add too much information, we might end up with a theory that overgenerates commitments. The most extreme outcome is a *trivial* theory that is committed to everything whatsoever.

**Concept. (Trivial Theory)** A theory that validly implies everything.

Triviality is extremely bad. Since a trivial theory has indiscriminate implications, it cannot be true (on pain of everything being true). The source of this defect is the internal structure of the theory itself. For this reason, trivial theories are widely considered to be the paradigm examples of nonsensical or uninterpretable theories.

The boundary between trivial and non-trivial theories indicates a difference between minimally acceptable theories and useless, nonsensical theories. Since this depends on logic, we can compare how different logics categorize trivial theories. This is one more way to compare and contrast different logical systems.

## 1.3 Proof Theory

In this section, we will briefly explore proof theory. We will only discuss propositional logics with a standard set of connectives as indicated in Section 1.2. We will highlight some details of proof theory for classical, intuitionistic, and relevant logics.

Proof theory gives a precise definition of derivations. A derivation might look like a list or a graph with formulas written at each step and transitions determined by the proof rules of the system. If we can construct a derivation that leads from the premise formulas $p_1, p_2, \ldots$ to the conclusion $q$, we write something like this:

$$p_1, p_2, \ldots \vdash q.$$

The single turnstile $\vdash$ is a symbol for the proof-theoretic definition of validity. The preceding displayed string says "from $p_1, p_2, \ldots$ it is valid to infer $q$." However, different logics give different theories of validity. So, we usually add a subscript L to the turnstile $\vdash_L$ and read this as saying "…it is valid according to logic L…."

There are a few styles of proof theory. For now, we will look at an approach that was popularized by the mathematician David Hilbert. This name will come up again in one important connection to eclectic pluralism (Section 2.6). In a Hilbert system, each derivation is a numbered list of formulas. It looks something like this:

| 1. | *Formula #1* | [Rule-Application #1] |
| 2. | *Formula #2* | [Rule-Application #2] |
| 3. | *Formula #3* | [Rule-Application #3] |

Each step contains a specific formula. On the right side, we list the *justification* of each step. The justification comes from the proof rules of the system. We are only allowed to make a step if it is somehow permitted by those rules.

Hilbert systems have several rules. One type of rule is a "proper" rule in the sense that it takes input from earlier steps of a derivation. We will look at one such proper rule known as *modus ponens*. This rule is a part of the proof theory for many logics.

- **Rule of Modus Ponens** Suppose you are building a derivation. At step $n$ you have the formula $p \rightarrow q$. At step $m$ you have the formula $p$. Then you are allowed to write $q$ at the next step with justification [MP, $n$, $m$]. This says that you reached the current step by applying *modus ponens (MP)* to the input steps $n$ and $m$.

It is important to understand that $p$ and $q$ can be replaced by any two formulas. The pattern is what matters. For example, the formulas $(p \vee s) \to r$ and $p \vee s$ could be input formulas. Modus ponens would then give us $r$ as output. The formulas $(p \to q) \to (s \to t)$ and $p \to q$ could be input formulas. Modus ponens would then give us $s \to t$ as output.

We need earlier steps in a derivation in order to generate later steps using MP, so where do the earlier steps come from? Some rules directly permit us to write down certain formulas. One of these rules just tells us that if we are reasoning with a particular premise, we can write that premise down at any time in our derivation.

- **Rule of Assumptions** If you are trying to derive something from premise $p$, you are allowed to write down $p$ at any step and mark it as an [Assumption].

Another important rule deals with formulas called *axioms*. Every Hilbert system comes with its own distinct set of axioms. They act as "free" pieces of information for derivations. The axioms of system L are the main engine of derivations in L.

- **Rule of Axioms** If there is an axiom called Axiom-A, then you are allowed to write down this kind of formula at any step with the justification [Axiom-A].

Now, this is all very abstract and we would perhaps like to know more about why these rules are chosen. Most especially, what are axioms? Why are some formulas chosen as axioms while others are not?

A helpful perspective, known as *inferentialism*, says that the meaning of an expression is determined by the inferences we may draw from sentences using that expression (Brandom, 1994; Dummett, 1991). For example, MP seems to capture an important aspect of the meaning of the conditional insofar as it permits the following step of reasoning: When you assert "If $p$, then $q$" and you assert $p$, you may infer $q$. In this spirit, axioms are often taken to be the forms of *analytic* sentences. Since the axioms of a logical system are what enable certain steps of reasoning, they also reflect a theory of meaning about the logical connectives in those axioms. For the time being, we leave this philosophical issue aside, but it will come up again in Sections 2.5 and 3.3.

Turning now to specific formal systems, we will first look at a set of axioms involving conjunction and disjunction. When we look at the Hilbert systems for classical, intuitionistic, and relevant logic, all three of them accept Ax1–Ax4.

**Definition. (Axioms for $\wedge$ and $\vee$)**

[Ax1] $(p \wedge q) \to p$
[Ax2] $(p \wedge q) \to q$

[Ax3] $p \to (p \vee q)$
[Ax4] $q \to (p \vee q)$

To be a bit more careful, these are technically *axiom schemata*. If we take a schema and uniformly replace the occurrences of each sentence letter ($p, q$, etc.) with any formula, then we have an axiom. Any formula that follows the pattern of one of the schemata counts as an axiom. For example, here are three different formulas that follow the pattern of Ax1: $(s \wedge t) \to s$, $((p \vee q) \wedge r) \to (p \vee q)$, $(p \wedge (r \to q)) \to p$. If we are working in a Hilbert system that accepts Ax1, then we are allowed to write down any of those formulas at any time.

Classical logic is the most widely taught logic. It is what you will find in most logic textbooks. The influence of classical logic on contemporary philosophy can be traced back to two philosophical mathematicians, Gottlob Frege (1879) and Bertrand Russell (1903). We write $\vdash_{CL}$ for derivability in classical logic. This is defined as follows.

**Definition. (Classical Derivability)** $p_1, p_2 \ldots \vdash_{CL} q$ means that, in the Hilbert system for classical logic, it is possible to construct a derivation where each premise $p_i$ is marked with [Assumption], the other steps of the derivation come from the classical axioms or from MP, and the final step is the conclusion formula $q$.

Since classical logic accepts Ax1–Ax4, we can show that $p \wedge q \vdash_{CL} q \vee r$.

| | | |
|---|---|---|
| 1. | $p \wedge q$ | [Assumption] |
| 2. | $(p \wedge q) \to q$ | [Ax2] |
| 3. | $q$ | [MP, 1, 2] |
| 4. | $q \to (q \vee r)$ | [Ax3] |
| 5. | $q \vee r$ | [MP, 3, 4] |

There is one premise $p \wedge q$, correctly marked with [Assumption]. The other steps in the derivation come from classical axioms or from MP. This meets all of the requirements for a classical derivation. It shows that the argument is classically derivable.

To give a complete Hilbert system for classical logic we need to fill in more axioms. We are not going to worry about completeness, but we will look at a few interesting classical axioms involving negation and (embedded) conditionals.

**Definition. (Classical Axioms for $\neg$ and $\to$)**

[Ax5] $(p \to (p \to q)) \to (p \to q)$
[Ax6] $(p \to q) \to ((q \to r) \to (p \to r))$
[Ax7] $p \to (q \to p)$

[Ax8] $p \to (\neg p \to q)$
[Ax9] $(p \to \neg q) \to (q \to \neg p)$
[Ax10] $(p \to \neg p) \to \neg p$
[Ax11] $\neg\neg p \to p$

With Ax7 we can use any formula of the form "If $p$, then if $q$, then $p$," and with Ax11, we can use any formula of the form "If not-not-$p$, then $p$." The second principle is known as *double negation elimination* (DNE). What can we do with these axioms?

Here is a derivation to show that $p \vdash_{CL} \neg\neg p$.

| | | |
|---|---|---|
| 1. | $p$ | [Assumption] |
| 2. | $(\neg p \to (\neg p \to \neg p)) \to (\neg p \to \neg p)$ | [Ax5] |
| 3. | $\neg p \to (\neg p \to \neg p)$ | [Ax7] |
| 4. | $\neg p \to \neg p$ | [MP, 1, 2] |
| 5. | $(\neg p \to \neg p) \to (p \to \neg\neg p)$ | [Ax9] |
| 6. | $p \to \neg\neg p$ | [MP, 4, 5] |
| 7. | $\neg\neg p$ | [MP, 1, 6] |

This is the principle of *double negation introduction* (DNI). Since classical logic accepts both DNI and DNE, it treats "not-not-$p$" as logically equivalent to $p$. In other words, it considers these two sentences to be able to prove all the same things.

We can show that $p \land \neg p \vdash_{CL} q$ as follows.

| | | |
|---|---|---|
| 1. | $p \land \neg p$ | [Assumption] |
| 2. | $(p \land \neg p) \to p$ | [Ax1] |
| 3. | $p$ | [MP, 1, 2] |
| 4. | $p \to (\neg p \to q)$ | [Ax8] |
| 5. | $\neg p \to q$ | [MP, 3, 4] |
| 6. | $(p \land \neg p) \to \neg p$ | [Ax2] |
| 7. | $\neg p$ | [MP, 1, 6] |
| 8. | $q$ | [MP, 5, 7] |

This is the principle of *explosion*, often expressed in Latin as *ex contradictione quodlibet*, which describes the inference pattern: from a contradiction, anything follows. Classical and intuitionistic logic both have explosive consequence relations, though not all logics possess this feature. Those who accept contradictions, but don't want their theories to be trivial, or who do not think that everything follows from a contradiction, will instead opt for a logic with a nonexplosive consequence relation.

There is a another classical principle $p \vdash_{CL} q \vee \neg q$ that looks like explosion flipped upside down. This is the principle of *excluded middle*. It captures the idea that either $q$ or $\neg q$ must hold come what may. The derivation of excluded middle is complicated. We will just sketch two components that make it work. For the first component, we can use Ax5–Ax9 to derive $\neg(q \vee \neg q) \to \neg q$ and then $\neg q \to \neg\neg(q \vee \neg q)$, then use Ax6 and Ax10 to derive $\neg\neg(q \vee \neg q)$. From here, Ax11 aka DNE gives us the conclusion $q \vee \neg q$. For the second component, we observe that this reasoning only appeals to axioms so we can correctly repeat the same steps under any assumption. These two components explain why $q \vee \neg q$ is derivable from any premise $p$ according to classical logic.

This particular example is a perfect derivation to highlight how *intuitionistic logic* and *relevant logic* diverge from classical logic. Both of these logics reject the derivation of excluded middle that we just explained, but for different reasons.

Intuitionistic logic is sometimes motivated by a background view on the nature of mathematics. L.E.J. Brouwer (1908) considered mathematics to depend on a mental activity that he called *construction*. For example, if you think about the concepts of a natural number and the less-than relation, pick any number, and keep reducing by one less, you will eventually reach 0. This construction results in a specific object that demonstrates the theorem "there is a smallest natural number." For a negative mathematical statement to hold $\neg p$, we must be able to perform a special construction: We must be able to *refute $p$* by showing that *every* method of trying to construct *$p$ fails*.

From this perspective, double negation elimination and excluded middle are questionable. Consider the following argument about a mathematical quantity used in the study of prime numbers known as Legendre's constant (L). Remember that "irrational number" is just an abbreviation for the expression "not a rational number."

---

**Example 8**

(8.1) Suppose that L is irrational.
(8.2) Then 1/2 is irrational, which is absurd.
∴ L is *not-not*-rational.

---

You don't need a lot of mathematics to understand this example. All you need to know is that (8.1) really does mathematically imply (8.2). Since the assumption "$\neg$(L is rational)" leads to absurd results, the conclusion "$\neg\neg$(L is rational)" follows. Both classical logic and intuitionistic logic can agree on those steps.

Double negation elimination would allow us to go further and infer "L is rational," but this is unwarranted from an intuitionistic perspective. Example 8 just shows that we can refute ($\neg$) every method of trying to refute ($\neg$) "L is rational." That is *different* from giving a construction of "L is rational." To reach that conclusion, we need to know the value of L, which our argument has not yet shown. These ideas about logical principles were implemented in a modern, formal system by Arendt Heyting (1930).

We can build a Hilbert system for intuitionistic logic with the following axioms for negation and (embedded) conditionals. Notice, these are mostly the same as the set of classical axioms. The only difference is that we removed Ax11 aka DNE.

**Definition. (Intuitionistic Axioms for $\neg$ and $\to$)**
[Ax5] $(p \to (p \to q)) \to (p \to q)$
[Ax6] $(p \to q) \to ((q \to r) \to (p \to r))$
[Ax7] $p \to (q \to p)$
[Ax8] $p \to (\neg p \to q)$
[Ax9] $(p \to \neg q) \to (q \to \neg p)$
[Ax10] $(p \to \neg p) \to \neg p$

The symbol for derivability in intuitionistic logic $\vdash_{IL}$ is defined as follows.

**Definition. (Intuitionistic Derivability)** $p_1, p_2 \ldots \vdash_{IL} q$ means that, in the Hilbert system for intuitionistic logic, it is possible to construct a derivation where each premise $p_i$ is marked with [Assumption], the other steps of the derivation come from the intuitionistic axioms or from MP, and the final step is the conclusion formula $q$.

Since intuitionistic logic accepts Ax1–Ax10 and otherwise has exactly the same rules as classical logic, many of the derivations we gave earlier are still acceptable. For example, we still have $p \wedge q \vdash_{IL} q \vee r$. We still have double negation introduction $p \vdash_{IL} \neg\neg p$ in intuitionistic logic. And we have the principle of explosion $p \wedge \neg p \vdash_{IL} q$. There is substantial overlap between intuitionistic logic and classical logic.

Unsurprisingly, the principle of excluded middle fails here $p \nvdash_{IL} q \vee \neg q$. Remember that the classical derivation of this result has two components. The first component is a series of steps using only axioms. We can still use Ax5–Ax10 to derive $\neg\neg(q \vee \neg q)$. However, we cannot derive $q \vee \neg q$ because we can't use DNE. That is why the derivation of excluded middle fails in intuitionistic logic. Any logical system that considers excluded middle to be invalid is called a *paracomplete* logic. Intuitionistic logic is the most famous example.

There is a systematic relationship between intuitionistic and classical logic. In a complete Hilbert system for intuitionistic logic, the rules are a proper subset of the rules for classical logic. The only difference is in the axioms. This means that any intuitionistic derivation has to be acceptable from the classical point of view:

$$p_1, p_2, \ldots \vdash_{IL} q \implies p_1, p_2, \ldots \vdash_{CL} q.$$

It does not work the other way around:

$$p_1, p_2, \ldots \vdash_{CL} q \not\implies p_1, p_2, \ldots \vdash_{IL} q.$$

That means that, in classical logic, we can often derive more conclusions from a certain set of premises assumptions than we can using intuitionistic logic. For this reason we say that intuitionistic logic is *weaker* than classical logic.

Finally, we will look at a Hilbert system for relevant logic. This type of logic is motivated by the view that explosion and excluded middle are degenerate forms of reasoning. These arguments look as if they pull unrelated sentences out of thin air. For example, here is an argument in plain English that has the form of explosion.

---

**Example 9**

(9.1) Jan is hungry.
(9.2) Jan is not hungry.
(9.3) ∴. The moon is made of green cheese.

---

Imagine that Jan is on the fence about having lunch. He can't make up his mind and he says, "I'm hungry, but then again I'm not." Your friend overhears this and jumps in with the remark, "Ah ha! That implies that the moon is made of green cheese!" Classical logic tells us that that this argument is valid, but relevant logics disagree.

This example is kind of silly, but it highlights an important point. Although the premises of this argument contradict each other, it is even more noticeable that the conclusion talks about a topic that has nothing to do with those premises. How could a claim about the moon follow from claims that only talk about Jan? The inventors of relevant logic, Anderson and Belnap (1962, 1975), claim that this kind of argument is invalid because the premises are *irrelevant* to the conclusion.

There are two aspects of a Hilbert system that formalize the notion of relevance. First, we go back to the classical axioms and remove Ax7 and Ax8 that generate classical derivations like $p, q \vdash_{CL} p$. We replace these axioms with a much simpler Ax12.

**Definition. (Relevant Axioms for ¬ and →)**

[Ax5] $(p \to (p \to q)) \to (p \to q)$
[Ax6] $(p \to q) \to ((q \to r) \to (p \to r))$

# Logical Pluralism

[Ax9] $(p \to \neg q) \to (q \to \neg p)$
[Ax10] $(p \to \neg p) \to \neg p$
[Ax11] $\neg\neg p \to p$
[Ax12] $p \to p$

Next, we will define an extra rule that basically says: Every assumption in a derivation must be used at some point, otherwise the derivation fails. All of this imposes a tight connection between sentences. The only acceptable derivations are those where the premises and conclusion have shared parts or shared content.

To formulate the extra rule for this Hilbert system, we can introduce a practice of *flagging* assumptions. A flag is a symbol. It could be anything. We attach a flag to each marked [Assumption]. In the following examples we use ♯ to stand for a flag. When we apply MP we pass any flags from inputs to outputs. The conclusion of a derivation must inherit a flag from each assumption, otherwise we have unused assumptions.

- **Rule of Relevance**: Each time you mark an [Assumption] you must *flag* it. Each time you use MP you must pass any flags from input formulas to the output formula. The final step of a derivation must have a flag from each [Assumption].

The symbol for derivability in relevant logic $\vdash_{RL}$ is defined as follows.

**Definition. (Relevant Derivability)** $p_1, p_2 \ldots \vdash_{RL} q$ means that, in the Hilbert system for relevant logic, it is possible to construct a derivation where each premise $p_i$ is marked with [Assumption], the other steps of the derivation come from the relevant axioms or from MP, the final step is the conclusion formula $q$, and the whole derivation satisfies the rule of relevance.

Here is a relevant derivation of $p \wedge q \vdash_{RL} q \vee r$.

| | | | | |
|---|---|---|---|---|
| 1. | $p \wedge q$ | [Assumption] | ♯ | |
| 2. | $(p \wedge q) \to q$ | [Ax2] | | |
| 3. | $q$ | [MP, 1, 2] | ♯ | |
| 4. | $q \to (q \vee r)$ | [Ax3] | | |
| 5. | $q \vee r$ | [MP, 3, 4] | ♯ | |

This looks almost exactly like the classical derivation. All of the axioms used in this derivation are accepted by both relevant and classical logic. The only extra detail is the column that keeps track of flags, which shows us that the derivation satisfies the rule of relevance, so it is completely acceptable in relevant logic.

Here is a relevant derivation of $p \vdash_{RL} \neg\neg p$.

| | | | |
|---|---|---|---|
| 1. | $p$ | [Ax12] | ♯ |
| 2. | $\neg p \to \neg p$ | [Ax12] | |
| 3. | $(\neg p \to \neg p) \to (p \to \neg\neg p)$ | [Ax8] | |
| 4. | $p \to \neg\neg p$ | [MP, 1, 2] | ♯ |
| 5. | $\neg\neg p$ | [MP, 1, 2] | ♯ |

Although the steps are slightly different from the classical derivation, the end result is the same. The flags show us that this derivation satisfies the rule of relevance. So, relevant logic accepts both DNI and DNE. It treats "not-not-$p$" as equivalent to $p$.

The classical derivation of explosion used Ax8, but there is no way to reach a similar result in relevant logic $p \wedge \neg p \not\vdash_{RL} q$. Any logical system that considers explosion to be invalid is called a *paraconsistent* logic. Relevant logic is the most famous example.

More interesting is why excluded middle fails $p \not\vdash_{RL} q \vee \neg q$. We used two components to explain the classical derivation. First, we explained how to derive $q \vee \neg q$ using axioms. Second, we notice that it is innocent to repeat those derivation steps under any assumption. In relevant logic, the second component is wrong. Suppose we start with a flagged assumption $p$. Then we introduce a bunch of axioms like $q \to (q \vee \neg q)$ or $\neg(q \vee \neg q) \to \neg(q \vee \neg q)$. This eventually leads to $q \vee \neg q$, but the final step only depended on the $q$-based axioms and not on the initial assumption $p$. The flag from $p$ will never be passed down, so this "attempted" derivation violates the rule of relevance.

In a complete Hilbert system for relevant logic, the axioms are a proper subset of the axioms for classical logic (Ax12 can be derived from Ax5 and Ax7). The main difference is the extra rule of relevance, which filters out a bunch of classical derivations. This means that any relevant derivation has to be acceptable from the classical point of view:

$p_1, p_2, \ldots \vdash_{RL} q \implies p_1, p_2, \ldots \vdash_{CL} q.$

It does not work the other way around:

$p_1, p_2, \ldots \vdash_{CL} q \not\implies p_1, p_2, \ldots \vdash_{RL} q.$

That means that, in classical logic, we can often derive more conclusions from a certain set of premises assumptions than we can using relevant logic. For this reason we say that relevant logic is *weaker* than classical logic.

That wraps up our discussion of proof theory for now. Hopefully, this section clearly illustrated the kind of methods that are unique to proof theory. You can find a summary of key result in Section 1.5. We will now turn to a different formal technique.

## 1.4 Model Theory

In this section, we will briefly present the model theory for classical, intuitionistic, and relevant propositional logics. On the model-theoretic approach, logic has an important connection with external phenomena like truth or verification.

Model theory gives a precise definition of abstract structures that we call semantic models. Each model represents a circumstance where someone might be reasoning. Formulas receive *semantic values*: 1 stands for true or verified and 0 stands for false or unverified. If it always happens (in every model) that when the premises $p_1, p_2, \ldots$ receive value 1, the conclusion $q$ also receives value 1, we write something like the following:

$$p_1, p_2, \ldots \vDash q.$$

The double turnstile $\vDash$ is a symbol for the model-theoretic definition of validity. The displayed string says "from $p_1, p_2, \ldots$ it is valid to infer $q$." However, different logics give different theories of validity. So, we add a subscript L to the turnstile $\vDash_L$ and read this as saying "…it is valid according to logic L.…"

Model theory treats validity as the *preservation* of truth or verification. On this approach, valid arguments are airtight because the conclusion "automatically" comes out true whenever the premises are true. This is why valid reasoning cannot go wrong.

In proof theory, the choice of axioms and rules made all the difference. Model theory has a similar feature, which we call *evaluation policies* (and supporting "apparatus"). This is sometimes connected to philosophy of mind and language, where sentence meaning has been identified as a set of *truth-conditions* (Heim and Kratzer, 1998). The idea behind truth-conditional semantics is that certain details determine the semantic values of complex sentences in any circumstance. However, to pose a challenging question: What are the circumstances in which a conditional sentence "If $p$, then $q$" is true? The value of $p$ might be important and the value of $q$ might be important, but is that enough information about a circumstance to tell us whether the conditional sentence is true? Different model theories offer very different answers to this question.

Classical logic has a truth-functional model theory. A model $M$ is literally built from a mathematical function $[\![.]\!]^M$ that maps certain inputs to outputs. The input side is always a formula and the output side is one of the semantic values, 1 or 0. The outputs represent the facts – what is true and what is false – in the circumstance represented by $M$:

$[\![p]\!]^M = 1$ says that $p$ is true in $M$.

$[\![p]\!]^M = 0$ says that $p$ is false in $M$.

The evaluation policies for complex formulas are also based on this simple representation of facts in a model. Classical models, thus, suggest the idea that "truth here and now" is the only thing about a circumstance that matters to logic.

When we state evaluation policies we write "iff" as an abbreviation for the ordinary English phrase "if and only if," which is an expression of definitional equivalence. The following policies tell us how conjunction and disjunction formulas are evaluated in classical logic. Much like we saw with proof theory, the classical treatment of conjunction and disjunction will carry over to other logics in this section.

**Definition. (Classical Evaluation of ∧ and ∨)** For any formula built from ∧ or ∨, a classical model $M$ must assign semantic values based on the following policies:

$[\![p \wedge q]\!]^M = 1$ iff both $[\![p]\!]^M = 1$ and $[\![q]\!]^M = 1$.
$[\![p \vee q]\!]^M = 1$ iff either $[\![p]\!]^M = 1$ or $[\![q]\!]^M = 1$.

We can read these policies as follows: A true conjunction requires both of its parts to be true, whereas a true disjunction requires only one of its parts to be true.

Once we have defined the range of classical models, then the symbol for semantically valid arguments in classical logic $\vDash_{CL}$ can be defined as follows:

**Definition. (Classical Semantic Validity)** $p_1, p_2 \ldots \vDash_{CL} q$ means that, in all classical models $M$, if $[\![p_1]\!]^M = 1$ and $[\![p_2]\!]^M = 1$ and…, then $[\![q]\!]^M = 1$.

For example, based on just the preceding details, we can easily see that $p \wedge q \vDash_{CL} q \vee r$. Just think about how the evaluation policies work in classical models. Consider any classical model $M$ where $[\![p \wedge q]\!]^M = 1$. Then we must have $[\![q]\!]^M = 1$ by the conjunction policy. So, we must have $[\![q \vee r]\!]^M = 1$ by the disjunction policy.

The most interesting question is how to handle negation and the conditional. For negation, we swap values. In any classical model, "not-*p*" has the opposite value from "*p*." For the conditional, we adopt something called the *material conditional*. According to this concept, the conditional sentence "if *p*, then *q*" has the same value as "not-*p* or *q*."

The material conditional treats an "if" statement as a statement purely about the facts here and now. Are there good reasons to do this? Here is an argument: The only type of circumstance that obviously falsifies "if *p*, then *q*" is a circumstance where *p* is true and *q* is false, so any other circumstance must make the sentence "if *p*, then *q*" true. If we accept that argument, then we will accept the following classical evaluation policies.

**Definition. (Classical Evaluation of $\neg$ and $\rightarrow$)** For any formula built from $\neg$ or $\rightarrow$, a classical model $M$ must assign semantic values based on the following policies:

$[\![\neg p]\!]^M = 1$ iff $[\![p]\!]^M = 0$.

$[\![p \rightarrow q]\!]^M = 1$ iff either $[\![p]\!]^M = 0$ or $[\![q]\!]^M = 1$.

With these definitions in place, we can check several argument forms we have not seen before. The following are called DeMorgan principles: $\neg(p \wedge q) \vDash_{CL} \neg p \vee \neg q$ and $\neg p \wedge \neg q \vDash_{CL} \neg(p \vee q)$ and $\neg(p \vee q) \vDash_{CL} \neg p \wedge \neg q$ and $\neg p \vee \neg q \vDash_{CL} \neg(p \wedge q)$.

Here is an explanation for the first DeMorgan principle. Take any classical model $M$. Suppose that $[\![\neg(p \wedge q)]\!]^M = 1$. Then we have $[\![p \wedge q]\!]^M = 0$. And that means either $[\![p]\!]^M = 0$ or $[\![p]\!]^M = 0$. So, we have $[\![\neg p]\!]^M = 1$ or $[\![\neg q]\!]^M = 1$. Thus, $[\![\neg p \vee \neg q]\!]^M = 1$. Similar explanations work for the other DeMorgan principles.

Each classical axiom in Section 1.3 is true in every classical model. For example, you can check for yourself that we always have $[\![(p \rightarrow (p \rightarrow q)) \rightarrow (p \rightarrow q)]\!]^M = 1$ and $[\![p \rightarrow (q \rightarrow p)]\!]^M = 1$ and $[\![(p \rightarrow \neg p) \rightarrow \neg p]\!]^M = 1$ in every model $M$.

If we look at the classically derivable arguments in Section 1.3, we can see that they are all semantically valid as well. For example, double negation elimination $\neg\neg p \vDash_{CL} p$, double negation introduction $p \vDash_{CL} \neg\neg p$, the principles of explosion $p \wedge \neg p \vDash_{CL} q$, and excluded middle $p \vDash_{CL} q \vee \neg q$. An *invalid* argument requires at least one model where the premises are true and the conclusion is untrue (a *countermodel*). The classical definition of negation guarantees that $[\![p \wedge \neg p]\!]^M = 0$ in every model $M$ so there is no countermodel for explosion. The definition of negation also guarantees that $[\![q \vee \neg q]\!]^M = 1$ in every model $M$ so there is no countermodel for excluded middle. With no countermodel, these arguments are considered valid in classical logic.

This is a good example to highlight how *intuitionistic logic* and *relevant logic* diverge from classical logic in their model theory just as much as their proof theory. Both of these logics reject excluded middle, but for different reasons.

As mentioned in Section 1.3, a historic motivation for intuitionistic logic was the idea that mathematics depends on creative thinking (mental construction). This idea has been modified and extended into a more general account of truth that can hold in many domains (Dummett, 1959; Wright, 1992). On this view, truth is said to be epistemically constrained: In some sense, what we cannot know cannot be true. Logical principles like excluded middle fail because negation is tied to such epistemic limitations.

We can build models that capture these intuitionistic ideas, but we need a more complex apparatus than before. Each model comes with a set of items $@, s_1, s_2, s_3, \ldots$ that represent potential *stages* in a creative thinking process. $@$ is the current stage of knowledge. There is a function $[\![.]\!]^M_s$ for each stage $s$ that maps formulas to 1 or 0. The output tells us the facts – what is verified and what is unverified – at each individual stage within the overall picture represented by model $M$:

$[\![p]\!]^M_s = 1$ says that $p$ is verified-at-$s$ in $M$.

$[\![p]\!]^M_s = 0$ says that $p$ is unverified-at-$s$ in $M$.

The evaluation policies for conjunction and disjunction look familiar.

**Definition. (Intuitionistic Evaluation of $\wedge$ and $\vee$)** For any formula built from $\wedge$ or $\vee$, an intuitionistic model $M$ must assign semantic values at each stage $s$ based on the following policies:

$[\![p \wedge q]\!]^M_s = 1$ iff both $[\![p]\!]^M_s = 1$ and $[\![q]\!]^M_s = 1$.

$[\![p \wedge q]\!]^M_s = 1$ iff either $[\![p]\!]^M_s = 1$ or $[\![q]\!]^M_s = 1$.

Importantly, stages are related to one another. $s_1 \prec s_2$ means that $s_1$ is *included* in $s_2$. This is meant to portray how knowledge can develop across potential stages, but always builds upon itself. In more abstract terms, we say that inclusion is:

- **Pointed**: Every stage includes the actual stage. (We always have $@ \prec s$.)
- **Reflexive**: Every stage includes itself. (We always have $s \prec s$.)
- **Transitive**: Inclusions persist over inclusions. (If $s_1 \prec s_2$ and $s_2 \prec s_3$, then $s_1 \prec s_3$.)
- **Cumulative**: Everything that is verified at an earlier stage continues to be verified at later stages in which it is included. (If $[\![p]\!]^M_{s_1} = 1$ and $s_1 \prec s_2$, then $[\![p]\!]^M_{s_2} = 1$.)

This relation forms a tree-like structure branching out from $@$, where every stage includes the facts that are known at $@$, but it can also add more facts. This suggests the notion of "truth unfolding through a creative thinking process" as a means of understanding logical properties. Notice, a single model or single picture of a circumstance now includes a whole structure of stages. This is important to negation and conditional formulas.

**Definition. (Intuitionistic Evaluation of $\neg$ and $\rightarrow$)** For any formula built from $\neg$ or $\rightarrow$, an intuitionistic model $M$ must assign semantic values at each stage $s$ based on the following policies:

## Logical Pluralism 23

$[\![\neg p]\!]_s^M = 1$ iff for all $s'$ such that $s \prec s'$, we have $[\![p]\!]_{s'}^M = 0$.

$[\![p \to q]\!]_s^M = 1$ iff for all $s'$ such that $s \prec s'$, if $[\![p]\!]_{s'}^M = 1$, then $[\![q]\!]_{s'}^M = 1$.

Informally, $\neg p$ is verified when there is no further, potential stage that verifies $p$. So, negation expresses refutability. The conditional $p \to q$ is verified when, at all further, potential stages of knowledge, if $p$ is verified, then $q$ is verified.

The symbol for intuitionistically valid arguments $\vDash_{IL}$ is defined as follows.

**Definition. (Intuitionistic Semantic Validity)** $p_1, p_2 \ldots \vDash_{IL} q$ means that, in all intuitionistic models $M$ and for all stages of the model $s$, if $[\![p_1]\!]_s^M = 1$ and $[\![p_2]\!]_s^M = 1$ and..., then $[\![q]\!]_s^M = 1$.

We can check a few important results of this definition.

Each of the intuitionistic axioms in Section 1.3 is verified at all stages of intuitionistic models. This relies on features of the inclusion relation. For example, $[\![p \to (q \to p)]\!]_s^M = 1$ always holds because of the cumulative feature of inclusion.

If we look at the intuitionisticly derivable arguments in Section 1.3, they are all semantically valid here. For example, the principle of explosion $p \land \neg p \vDash_{IL} q$ holds because the premises can never be verified. The principle of double negation introduction $p \vDash_{IL} \neg\neg p$ may not be obvious. Consider this explanation. Take any model with $s$ where $[\![p]\!]_s^M = 1$, then $\neg p$ is forever unverified, which means that $[\![\neg\neg p]\!]_s^M = 1$. Why is $\neg p$ forever unverified? When $[\![p]\!]_s^M = 1$ and $s \prec s'$ we get $[\![p]\!]_{s'}^M = 1$ at all future stages, by reflexivity they all see that $p$ is not refutable, thus $[\![\neg p]\!]_{s'}^M = 0$ at all future stages.

The following diagram of an intuitionistic model helps us to see how this semantics invalidates DNE and excluded middle. Each dot is a stage. @ is on the far left. The formulas written above a stage are verified at that stage. The inclusion relation follows the arrows. In this model, $p$ is *not yet* verified by the initial stage $[\![p]\!]_@^M = 0$, but there is some later evolution of thought where $p$ *eventually* becomes verified.

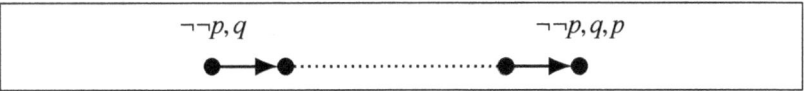

Call the ultimate stage $s$ where $[\![p]\!]_s^M = 1$. Because @ $\prec s$, we have $[\![\neg p]\!]_@^M = 0$. Since $[\![p]\!]_@^M = 0$, we have $[\![p \lor \neg p]\!]_@^M = 0$. This is a *countermodel* to excluded middle $q \nvDash_{IL} p \lor \neg p$. This model represents a circumstance where a potential, linear expansion of verified facts undermines the claim that $p$ must be verified or refuted (it is neither).

The preceding model exhibits a form of *coherent incompleteness*. It portrays the kind of circumstance where the current stage of knowledge "refutes the refutation of *p*" without verifying *p*. If we think that this portrays a genuine possible circumstance of reasoning, then we might agree with the intuitionistic logical principles.

A somewhat surprising feature of intuitionistic logic is that one of the DeMorgan principles fails in this logic: $\neg(p \wedge q) \not\vDash_{IL} \neg p \vee \neg q$. For a countermodel, just imagine a circumstance where there is a potential expansion of verified facts in two different branches. *p* is *not yet* verified but *eventually* becomes verified at the end of one branch, and *q* is *not yet* verified but *eventually* becomes verified at the end of a different branch. This results in $[\![\neg(p \vee q)]\!]^M_@ = 1$ and $[\![\neg p]\!]^M_@ = 0$ and $[\![\neg q]\!]^M_@ = 0$.

Finally, we will discuss a model theory for relevant logic. We will present a semantic framework where the *relevance requirement* is a byproduct of information flow between states of affairs (Restall, 1996; Mares, 2004).

One of the tools for this semantics is that we treat $[\![.]\!]$ as a loose relation instead of a strict function. Think of 1 and 0 as *independent* properties. The fact that there is no elephant in my apartment might be an example of a primitive, negative "non-elephant-ish" fact. It is independent from a list of all the positive facts about my apartment: the floors are made of wood, the walls are green, the windows are large, etc. If we use semantic values in this way, then a specific formula *p* might get the value 1, it might get 0, it might not get any value, it might even get both values at once. These options might represent something like incomplete or inconsistent entries in a database (Belnap, 1992).

Using this tool, we will build up relevant models. Each model comes with a set of items $@, s_1, s_2, s_3, \ldots$ that represent potential *states of affairs*. $@$ is the actual state. There is a loose relation $[\![.]\!]^M_s$ between each *s* and the semantic values 1 and 0:

$[\![p]\!]^M_s \cong 1$ says that *p* is true-at-*s* in *M*.

$[\![p]\!]^M_s \cong 0$ says that *p* is false-at-*s* in *M*.

The symbol $\cong$ means "at least has this value." The evaluation policies for conjunction and disjunction are familiar, but we have to write separate policies for each possible value.

**Definition. (Relevant Evaluation of $\wedge$ and $\vee$)** For any formula built from $\wedge$ or $\vee$, a relevant model *M* must assign semantic values at each state *s* based on the following policies:

$[\![p \wedge q]\!]^M_s \cong 1$ iff both $[\![p]\!]^M_s \cong 1$ and $[\![q]\!]^M_s \cong 1$.

$[\![p \wedge q]\!]^M_s \cong 0$ iff either $[\![p]\!]^M_s \cong 0$ or $[\![q]\!]^M_s \cong 0$.

$[\![p \vee q]\!]^M_s \cong 1$ iff either $[\![p]\!]^M_s \cong 1$ or $[\![q]\!]^M_s \cong 1$.

$[\![p \vee q]\!]^M_s \cong 0$ iff both $[\![p]\!]^M_s \cong 0$ and $[\![q]\!]^M_s \cong 0$.

States are related in relevant models. $s_1 s_2 \sqsupset s_3$ means that the information in $s_1$ and $s_2$ is *realized* in $s_3$. This portrays how states can be joined together to generate information that was not available in them separately.

Consider a realistic example: There was a state where Antoni Gaudí came up with a design such that, if it were funded, the Sagrada Família would be the most beautiful church in Barcelona, and there was a state in which the project was eventually funded, but the combination of these states was only realized later when the Sagrada Família was built and it really did became the most beautiful church in Barcelona. This productive relation creates *n-chains* of information with the following pattern:

$$s_1 s_2 \sqsupset x_1 \text{ and } x_1 s_3 \sqsupset x_2 \text{ and } \ldots \text{and } x_{(n-1)} s_n \sqsupset s_{(n+1)}.$$

When we have this kind of pattern in a model, we call the $s$ parts *sites* and we call the $x$ parts *channels* that together form an information chain from $s_1$ to $s_{(n+1)}$. Now, in abstract terms, we say that the realization relation is:

- **Pointed**: @ does not alter the information of any state (@$s \sqsupset s$).
- **Commutative**: the realization of two joined states does not depend on the order in which those states are joined together (whenever $s_1 s_2 \sqsupset s_3$, then $s_2 s_1 \sqsupset s_3$).
- **Extensible**: realization chains can always be extended through an intermediary channel (whenever $s_1 s_2 \sqsupset s_3$, there is some $x$ such that $s_1 s_2 \sqsupset x$ and $x s_2 \sqsupset s_3$).

This suggests the notion of "truth across information chains" as a means of understanding logical properties. Notice, a single model or single picture of a circumstance now includes a whole structure of states. This is important to negation and conditional formulas.

**Definition. (Relevant Evaluation of ¬ and →)** For any formula built from ¬ or →, a relevant model $M$ must assign semantic values at each state, $s$, based on the following policies:

$[\![ \neg p ]\!]_s^M \cong 1$ iff $[\![ p ]\!]_s^M \cong 0$.

$[\![ \neg p ]\!]_s^M \cong 0$ iff $[\![ p ]\!]_s^M \cong 1$.

$[\![ p \to q ]\!]_s^M \cong 1$ iff for all $s', s''$ such that $ss' \sqsupset s''$, if $[\![ p ]\!]_{s'}^M \cong 1$, then $[\![ q ]\!]_{s''}^M \cong 1$.

$[\![ p \to q ]\!]_s^M \cong 0$ iff for some $s', s''$ we have $s's'' \sqsupset s$ and $[\![ p ]\!]_{s'}^M \cong 1$ and $[\![ q ]\!]_{s''}^M \cong 0$.

Informally, $\neg p$ is true when $p$ is false, and vice versa. This is extremely similar to the classical definition. The relevant conditional $p \to q$ is evaluated by the realization relation. This makes perfect sense based on what we said earlier: $p \to q$ is true in the kind of states that can always be combined with $p$-states to realize $q$-states.

The symbol for relevantly valid arguments $\vDash_{\mathsf{RL}}$ is defined as follows.

**Definition. (Relevant Semantic Validity)** $p_1, p_2 \ldots \vDash_{RL} q$ means that, in all relevant models $M$ for all $n$-chains, $s_1 s_2 \sqsupset x_1$ and $x_1 s_3 \sqsupset x_2$ and ...and $x_{(n-1)} s_n \sqsupset s_{(n+1)}$, if $[\![p_1]\!]_{s_1}^M \cong 1$ and $[\![p_2]\!]_{s_2}^M \cong 1$ and..., then $[\![q]\!]_{s_{(n+1)}}^M \cong 1$.

This precisely defines valid arguments in terms of truth preservation across the sites of information chains. [*Technical Note:* The length of chains that matter depends on the premises in an argument. To be absolutely precise, we specify two special cases: a 0-chain only involves the actual state @, which reflects @@ $\sqsupset$ @, and a 1-chain involves @ and some state $s$, which reflects @$s \sqsupset s$.] We can now check a few results.

The majority of relevant axioms in Section 1.3 are true at @ (the 0-chain) in any relevant model. For example, $[\![p \to p]\!]_@^M = 1$ is always true because of pointedness. [*Technical Note:* It is only the *majority* of axioms because our models do not always make Ax9 and Ax10 true. Our proof theory is closer to the "standard" relevant logic known as R, but our model theory is closer to the "basic" relevant logic B. This makes the presentation simpler on both sides and the discrepancy between the proof theory and model theory makes no difference to the key results we want to highlight in this Element.]

If we look at the relevantly derivable arguments in Section 1.3, it is not difficult to see that they are all semantically valid: $\neg\neg p \vDash_{RL} p$ and $p \vDash_{RL} \neg\neg p$ hold, as do all of the DeMorgan principles $\neg(p \wedge q) \vDash_{CL} \neg p \vee \neg q$ and $\neg p \wedge \neg q \vDash_{CL} \neg(p \vee q)$ and $\neg(p \vee q) \vDash_{CL} \neg p \wedge \neg q$ and $\neg p \vee \neg q \vDash_{CL} \neg(p \wedge q)$.

Below is a diagram to indicate how this model theory imposes a requirement of shared parts in valid arguments. In the following diagram, each dot is a state. The lines represent the realization relation: The combination of two states on the left is realized in the state on the right. A formula with + has value 1, a formula with − has value 0, and a formula with ? has no value at that state. Imagine that $p$ stands for "this is a pig" and $q$ stands for "that is a quince." One sentence is about animals, the other sentence is about fruits. The pig state supports $p+$ all by itself but does *not* support $q+$ and the quince state supports $q+$ all by itself but does *not* support $p+$. When the combination of states is realized, we only get out positive information supported by *all states*.

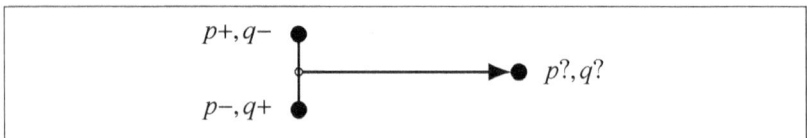

Call the first two states $s_1$ and $s_2$ and the third state $s_3$ so we have $s_1 s_2 \sqsupset s_3$. This model has a 2-chain where combined $p$ and $q$ information does not necessarily lead to $p$, which explains why $p, q \nvDash_{RL} p$. Since the combination of $s_1$ with a

$q$-state is not always realized in a $p$-state, we have $[\![q \to p]\!]^M_{s_1} \not\cong 1$. So, this model also has a 1-chain where $p$ information does not necessarily lead to $q \to p$, hence $p \nvDash_{\mathsf{RL}} q \to p$.

Finally, we can very quickly explain how explosion and excluded middle fail in this semantics. A state $s$ where $[\![p]\!]^M_s \cong 1$ and $[\![p]\!]^M_s \cong 0$ gives us $[\![p \land \neg p]\!]^M_s \cong 1$. We call this a *truth-glut*. If we also have that $[\![q]\!]^M_s$ is not related to any semantic value, then $[\![q \lor \neg q]\!]^M_s \not\cong 1$. We call this a *truth-gap*. This countermodel works precisely because $p \land \neg p$ does not have shared parts or shared content with $q \lor \neg q$.

The model we have just described exhibits a form of *coherent inconsistency*. Some people think that this can be motivated by the Liar paradox, "This very sentence is false." We may feel compelled to accept the Liar and its negation, but that doesn't mean we are ready to accept every random statement (Priest, 2006b; Beall, 2009). This reflects a difference between the classification of theories in relevant logic and our other systems of classical and intuitionistic logic. According to classical or intuitionistic logic, an inconsistent theory is *trivial*, but according to relevant logic, it is *non-trivial*.

It is worthwhile to mention that there is at least one more influential way of doing model theory. A *many-valued* semantics has additional semantic values beyond just 1 and 0. (The many-valued approach was invented by the Polish logician Jan Łukasiewicz and, as we will see in the next section, he considered many-valued logics to be important competitors to classical logic. For more on many-valued logics, you may consult the Cambridge Element *Many-Valued Logics* (2026).) To illustrate the idea, suppose we take $i$ to represent a third semantic value that is different from truth and falsity. We can give a truth-functional semantics in this way, as long as we explain the outputs for all values. Here is a common way of handling the evaluation policies for negation in a three-valued logic.

**Definition. (Three-valued Evaluation of $\neg$ and $\to$)** A model $M$ must assign semantic values based on the following policies:

$[\![\neg p]\!]^M = 1$ iff $[\![p]\!]^M = 0$.
$[\![\neg p]\!]^M = i$ iff $[\![p]\!]^M = i$.
$[\![\neg p]\!]^M = 0$ iff $[\![p]\!]^M = 1$.

Notice, when $p$ has the third value, so does its negation $\neg p$.

We group semantic values into *designated* ones and *undesignated* ones and define validity as the preservation of designated values. 1 is on the designated side and 0 is on the undesignated side, but there can be many interpretations of the extra values.

For example, we might have a three-valued model theory for paracomplete logic where the third value $i$ stands for the status "neither true nor false." The set of designated values just includes the standard value for truth $D = \{1\}$, but now we have different kinds of undesignated values $U = \{0, i\}$ because we can represent different ways of lacking truth. Without going fully into the details, this can give us a countermodel to excluded middle where $[\![p \vee \neg p]\!]^M \in U$ because $[\![p]\!]^M \in U$ and $[\![\neg p]\!]^M \in U$. This is a slightly different approach from the semantic methods for paracomplete logic that we studied before.

For one more example, we might have a three-valued model theory for paraconsistent logic where $i$ means "both true and false." The set of designated values is now $D = \{1, i\}$ because we can represent different ways of being true, but there is just one undesignated value $U = \{0\}$. Without going fully into the details, this can give us countermodels to explosion where $[\![p \wedge \neg p]\!]^M \in D$ because $[\![p]\!]^M \in D$ and $[\![\neg p]\!]^M \in D$. Again, this is different from the semantic methods for paraconsistent logic that we studied before.

That wraps up our discussion of model theory for now. To close this section, we will step back and review our key results with some additional commentary on how to think about similarities and differences between logics.

## 1.5 Summary

In this section, we took a whirlwind tour of formal logics. You may feel a bit lost in the details, so we will summarize and extend the most interesting observations.

Formal logics use a number of techniques to theorize validity. The aim is to give a precise, extensional definition of valid argument forms. One technique, proof theory, defines validity in terms of rule-following. Another technique, model theory, defines validity as preservation of important semantic values (truth or verification). There are a wide variety of logics that enjoy proof theory or model theory along the preceding lines. These logics all offer recognizable theories of validity, understood to be a formal and necessary (epistemically or metaphysically) property of arguments.

We focused mostly on classical, intuitionistic, and relevant propositional logics. These are just examples of formal logics, but these systems have been central to the debate over logical pluralism (this is, in part, simply because they were of interest to pluralists like Carnap, Beall, and Restall, but also because they have been fruitfully used in outside applications, e.g. in the foundations of mathematics). We looked at some ideas about how to develop a proof theory or model theory for each of these logics. These logics *completely agree* about a substantial number of valid argument forms.

$p \wedge q \vdash p$ ($\wedge$ elimination #1)
$p \wedge q \vdash q$ ($\wedge$ elimination #2)
$p \vdash p \vee q$ ($\vee$ introduction #1)
$q \vdash p \vee q$ ($\vee$ introduction #2)
$p \wedge (q \vee r) \vdash (p \wedge q) \vee (p \wedge r)$ ($\wedge$-$\vee$ distribution)
$p, p \rightarrow q \vdash q$ (MP from assumptions)
$p \vdash \neg\neg p$ ($\neg\neg$ introduction)
$\neg p \wedge \neg q \vdash \neg(p \vee q)$ (DeMorgan #1)
$\neg(p \vee q) \vdash \neg p \wedge \neg q$ (DeMorgan #2)
$\neg p \vee \neg q \vdash \neg(p \wedge q)$ (DeMorgan #3)

In proof theory, we saw how agreement between logics can be traced back to a large number of shared axioms and rules. In model theory, things look quite different on the surface, but note the following observation: If you take any of our non-classical models that has only a single point of evaluation @, it will look and behave just like a classical model. Each of these non-classical models can, thus, be seen as a generalization of some classical model. They are not as far apart as they seem to be.

On this basis, we can show that any argument form that has a countermodel in classical logic *also* has a countermodel in intuitionistic logic and relevant logic. This is a very quick sketch of the following relationship between semantic validity in our three logics:

$p_1, p_2, \ldots \vDash_{IL} q \implies p_1, p_2, \ldots \vDash_{CL} q.$
$p_1, p_2, \ldots \vDash_{RL} q \implies p_1, p_2, \ldots \vDash_{CL} q.$

Clearly, those relationships only hold in one direction. For more details on such technical results, you may want to consult a logic textbook like Priest (2008). This brings us to the question of how and why logics diverge.

Classical logic accepts the following principles:

$p \vdash q \rightarrow p$ (positive weakening)
$p \vdash \neg p \rightarrow q$ (negative weakening)
$p \wedge \neg p \vdash q$ (explosion)
$p \vdash q \vee \neg q$ (excluded middle)
$\neg\neg p \vdash p$ ($\neg\neg$ elimination)
$\neg(p \wedge q) \vdash \neg p \vee \neg q$ (DeMorgan #4)

Relevant logic rejects the first four items on this list. Intuitionistic logic rejects the last three. In proof theory, these differences can be traced back to different choices of axioms and rules. In model theory, the same kind of differences can be traced back to different choices of semantic apparatus and evaluation policies.

On a naive interpretation, these choices not only reflect distinct theories of validity, but also distinct theories of what *grounds* validity. This is indirectly tied up with different ways of drawing the boundary around trivial theories. Different logics may, thus, assume different views on rationality or meaning (inferential or truth-conditional). For all of these reasons, the differences between logics can appear to be deep and profound.

A good way to broach the topic of logical pluralism, then, is to think about the balance between these factors. What is more telling: The continuities or the differences between logics? Is there a subtle way in which apparent differences between logics can be reconciled and brought together under one umbrella? Why should we want that?

## 2 Pluralistic Perspectives

### 2.1 An Analogy

As we know, logical pluralism revolves around the following thesis:

**The Pluralist Thesis:** There is more than one correct logic.

In this section, we will explore arguments in support of the pluralist thesis. The central issue, as we understand it, is the notion of correctness for logic.

Pluralism is typically opposed to *logical monism*: the view that there is exactly one correct logic. Both monists and pluralists appeal to a notion of correctness in order to state their views. The category of correct logic is best seen as a philosophical category and not one that can simply be gleaned from observations of system building in formal logic. Monists and pluralists disagree about the scope of this category. A less widely discussed option is *logical nihilism*: the view that there are no correct logics.

When monists and pluralists discuss their views, they do not always speak of correct logic(s), but sometimes prefer to speak of *admissible, legitimate*, or *genuine* logic(s). In this Element, talk of correctness will stand in for any of these approbative terms. The basic outline of any pluralist view on logic involves a definition of correct logic and the claim that more than one logic satisfies the criteria for entry into this category.

There is a clear sense in which logical monism is the natural, default position in this debate. We expect questions about climate change or neuroscience to each have a single correct answer, so why not questions about logic? Łukasiewicz (1936, p. 233) expresses a kind of default monism when he says the following.

> I am convinced that one and only one of these logical systems …is real [Łukasiewicz himself only focuses on classical versus many-valued logics],

in the same way as one and only one system of geometry is real. Today, it is true, we do not yet know which system that is, but I do not doubt that empirical research will sometime demonstrate whether the space of the universe is Euclidean or non-Euclidean and whether relationships between facts correspond to two-valued logic or to one of the many-valued logics.

Historically, logicians who had an opinion on this matter were similarly inclined. Many logicians engaged with alternative logics in an exploratory manner, but the opinionated amongst them like Frege and Brouwer typically saw themselves as upholding correct beliefs on logic against the incorrect beliefs of their rivals. It would never have crossed their minds that both sides of the debate might be correct in their own ways.

In Section 1, we saw how different logics appear to involve deeply divided theories not only about the extensional definition of validity, but even its grounds. It is, therefore, quite important to ask: How could more than one logic be correct?

Simply put, logical pluralism invokes *parameterization*: The view that correctness for logic is not an absolute matter, but is sensitive to some hidden parameter that can be filled in more than one way. Shapiro (2014b, pp. 7–9) uses the label "folk-relativism" to refer to roughly the same idea. As we will see, pluralists say many different things about these parameters. For now, the point is that parametrically correct logics are correct for slightly different reasons and in slightly different ways. This at least promises to clarify the possibility that such logics are, in fact, compatible with one another.

Logical monism sometimes issues from nothing more than a firmly held belief that there must be a uniquely correct logic *by the very nature of logic*. Łukasiewicz's geometric analogy suggests something like this. He says that there are many geometric structures, but also external tie-breaking factors that give privileged status to one of these systems, and the same holds true for logic.

To unpack this a bit, what we call a geometric structure is a mathematical space equipped with points, lines, and a relation of *parallelism*. For any point $P$ that is not on line $L$ we can look for the lines that pass through $P$ without intersecting $L$. Call them parallel lines. In traditional Euclidean geometry there is exactly one parallel passing through any point off of a line. For centuries, mathematicians largely assumed that this was the only way to conceive of parallelism, but in the mid-nineteenth century we learned that this is not the case. We can define geometric axioms that express different conceptions of parallelism. For example, in hyperbolic geometry (spaces with negative curvature) there can be many parallels passing through the same point off of a line. This transformed the field of geometry into the study of different types of structures, each with their own internal definitions of the fundamental geometric relations.

This much is well known, but as soon as we ask what makes a geometric structure correct or incorrect, we are asking a philosophical question. Pure mathematics stops at the study of these abstract structures (though, of course, mathematicians may also have opinions about the philosophical interpretation of their field).

Łukasiewicz offers a plausible rubric to address this philosophical question. He appeals to facts about physical space as a criterion for correctness in geometry. The relationship between geometric structures and physics is historically significant, since the entire field of study has its genesis in inquiries about physical space. Priest (2006a) calls this the canonical application of geometry and he fully agrees with its philosophical role. A geometric structure is correct if it represents physical space. We can then make a strong case for geometric monism: the view that there is exactly one correct geometric system. Einstein's theory of special relativity is the best scientific theory of physical space. It is amongst the most secure scientific theories we have and it essentially relies on the framework of hyperbolic geometry. This is a sketch of a philosophical argument for the view that hyperbolic geometry is uniquely correct in the preceding sense.

Compelling as this may be, it needn't prejudice our views toward *logic* because the similarities between the two topics break down at a crucial point. Just like in geometry, we can make the case that logic has a canonical application that determines logical correctness (cf. Priest (2006a)). Logic has its genesis in inquiries about validity. A logical system is correct if it captures what is valid. Just like in geometry, we see that modern logical methods have produced many types of logical systems. The monist expects the canonical application of this field to play a tie-breaking role between logics, pointing us toward the uniquely correct system. Is she right about that?

At this point, the analogy with geometry is shaky. The canonical application of geometry has clear empirical content. We see physical space every day of our lives. Insofar as its applications in physics are decisive, the question of correct geometric structure has significant ties to one particular part of science. However, we cannot say the same about logic. The canonical application of logic does not have clear empirical content. We do not see what follows from what. Logic does not have a significant tie to one particular part of science. We cannot identify an independent theory whose content distinctively bears on the question of which logic is correct. None of this refutes monism, it just undermines the too-quick route to logical monism by way of a shaky analogy with geometry. We should not be nearly as confident about logical monism as we are about geometric monism. Nothing should prejudice us in advance against the very possibility of logical pluralism.

So, what positive arguments have been given for the pluralist thesis? There are two broad camps. Some pluralists start with particularly strong views about logical *methods*. They argue that, by design, logical systems do not perfectly represent the properties that are their intended targets. On this type of view, pluralism arises primarily from logical tools and methods. Other pluralists claim that correctness for logic exhibits a distinctive kind of *indeterminacy*. They argue that logics aim to fulfill an important, pre-theoretic concept, but it turns out that this can be accomplished in more than one way. On this type of view, pluralism arises from the nature of the logical phenomena.

- **Pluralism from Methodology:** Logics are flexible, epistemic tools. Any logic that serves its design goals is correct. Many logics serve their design goals.
- **Pluralism from Indeterminacy:** Some logical concept is indeterminate. Any logic that realizes this concept is correct. Many logics realize that concept.

These are not necessarily exclusive ideas about the source of pluralism. Some pluralists like Shapiro (2014b) seem to acknowledge both of these factors in some degree.

There are helpful parallels with the neighboring philosophical view of *alethic pluralism*. Just as we said about other topics, monism is the natural, default position when it comes to the nature of truth. However, advocates of alethic pluralism argue that the search for a single, unique property of truth is futile (Lynch, 2009; Wright, 2013).

One argument for this view revolves around value statements ("this is delicious"). These declarative statements might seem truth-apt even though they do not seem to correspond with any objective facts. The alethic pluralist accommodates this by positing that a different property realizes truth for value statements than for other statements. Correspondence with the facts only realizes truth in some discourse domains, but not all of them. This exemplifies a novel strategy: when the pluralist encounters a difficulty for orthodox theory (correspondence truth, or classical logic) she does not abandon the orthodoxy, but continues to accept it in a modified form *alongside rival theories*.

Alethic pluralists emphasize the need for unity in the study of truth, otherwise they cannot claim to have identified many instances of one phenomenon. Lynch and Wright rely on a distinction between concepts and properties: the concept of truth is one, its realizers are many. We said from the outset that a pluralist view should offer us a satisfying path between unity and plurality. Beall and Restall (2006) call this *constrained freedom*. They contend that the logical pluralist needs to bring unity to the phenomenon of correct logics, make room for more than one instance, but avoid saying that "anything goes." The limitations are just as important as the degrees of freedom because pluralism without limits does not yield a philosophically interesting point of view.

We start our discussion of pluralist views with Alfred Tarski and Rudolph Carnap. They both largely fall into the methodological camp along with Susan Haack who helped crystallize the contemporary formulation of logical pluralism.

## 2.2 The Roots of Pluralism

Tarski was born in Poland and trained in the Lvov-Warsaw school of logic, while Carnap was born in Germany and co-founded the Vienna Circle (the logical positivists). Both relocated to the US during World War II. They had complementary philosophical tastes. The views of one author influenced the other, and this influence flowed in both directions.

Tarski and Carnap both place great importance on the distinction between natural languages like English, Polish, or German and the artificial, formal languages used in logical studies. We introduced formal languages in Section 1.2 in a fairly common way: They are tools for representing formal structure that exists independently in natural language. Tarski and Carnap see things differently. They view a formal language as a novel and self-standing means of expression that does not necessarily line up with any informal means of expression. Concepts expressed in a formal language have explicit, precise definitions. They can be stipulated to avoid vagueness and ambiguity. For these reasons, a formal language will generally be a better vehicle for science than any natural language. Carnap calls this *explication*: the process of designing a formal language to replace the use of informal language in theoretical disciplines.

This creates distance between formal languages and our everyday intuitions about reasoning and communication. Formal tools are said to be productive because they are creative. This naturally leaves open the possibility of some degree of pluralism. This methodological outlook can be seen in several aspects of Tarski and Carnap's work.

An early and successful example of explication is found in Tarski's theory of truth. Tarski (1933, 1944) showed how to construct a formal theory that would preserve every instance of the following biconditional, where "$p$" is the name of sentence $p$.

**Concept. (Truth Schema)** "$p$" is true if, and only if $p$.

This principle says, roughly, that to assert a claim *about* the truth of a sentence is equivalent to simply asserting the sentence itself, which says something *about* the world. Although it may sound mundane, Tarski's theory hides several achievements. The first is that this theory avoids inconsistency by simply prohibiting the Liar sentence (see Section 1.4). This allows an unproblematic use of classical logic within this theory. The second achievement is that the truth schema does not appeal to any substantial metaphysical assumptions, pointing the way toward the deflationist theory of truth. This illustrates the productive potential of treating formal languages as self-standing objects of study.

Carnap (1937, 1950) develops a view about *existence* with a similar flavor. He starts from the broad view that every theory has its own linguistic framework constituted by voluntarily chosen rules. There are four different ways to think about existence questions relative to frameworks, only two of which admit interesting answers.

- *Internal* questions are answered within a framework.
  - General internal questions are totally unexciting. Consider a mathematical framework that includes the concepts of numbers and operations. The question "Are there numbers?" has a transparent answer in this framework ("yes!").
  - Specific internal questions, on the other hand, are slightly more interesting. To answer (or try to answer) the internal question "Are there prime numbers whose squares are not separated by at least four other primes?" we just prove (or try to prove) things within the rules of the framework.
- *External* questions are raised outside of a framework.
  - Some external questions can be interpreted as questions *about* frameworks, which are legitimate. When I ask about numbers in this way, I am really asking "Should I use a framework that includes the concept of numbers?" The answer is pragmatic: if it is fruitful for your purposes, then use it.
  - Finally, there are general questions asked with a skeptical tone from an external perspective. When the skeptic asks "Yes, but do numbers *really* exist?" their question is illegitimate, according to Carnap, because we have no clear method of resolving any debate about this question.

These distinctions are meant to dissuade us from certain traditional, interminable debates in philosophy. In particular, Carnap hopes to dissuade other philosophers from seeking out the "one true" logic. This topic brings in its tow an array of "pseudo-problems and wearisome controversies" (Carnap, 1937, p. xiv). In an infamous passage, he promotes a liberal proliferation of logics without need for competition.

> Our attitude to requirements of this kind is given a general formulation in the *Principle of Tolerance: It is not our business to set up prohibitions but to arrive at conventions....  In logic, there are no morals.* Everyone is at

liberty to build up his own logic, i.e. his own language. All that is required of him is that, if he wishes to discuss it, he must state his methods clearly, and give syntactical rules instead of philosophical arguments. (Carnap, 1937, pp. 51–52)

This is the spark that ignited the flame of logical pluralism.

We can build a Carnapian framework by using something like proof rules. This may or may not be a Hilbert system. The rules could extend well beyond the kind of logical rules we discussed in Section 1.4 to include also rules for non-logical expressions. If we approach science in this way, then the rules of our chosen framework determine the correct usage of expressions just like the rules of a game determine which moves are legal in that game. Once we state enough rules, we have fully determined what we can say and how we can reason in this framework.

Clearly, there is a great deal of flexibility in how frameworks could be designed. Tolerance goes a step further to enshrine an *in principle* permissive attitude toward such frameworks, especially their basic logical rules. It asserts that no logic is completely off the table. No set of logical rules is self-evidently correct. In fact, Carnap derides talk of correctness in logic: "The first attempts to cast the ship of logic off from the *terra firma* of the classical forms were certainly bold…But they were hampered by the striving after 'correctness'." (Carnap, 1937, p. xv). He views the issue of correctness in logic as being akin to an illegitimate, external question about existence. It is pointless to ask about it because we have no clear method of resolving such questions.

Nonetheless, we should call Carnap a kind of logical pluralist. He would agree that there is more than one way to answer pragmatic questions about whether a logic is useful to a specific kind of theory. Carnap himself explored mathematical frameworks developed using classical logic and those using an intuitionistic, constructive logic. He can view logical laws just like he views internal, general existence claims: A set of logical laws hold internal to a framework and the question of their correctness has a transparent answer within that framework. If the rules determine that a given argument is valid, then it is internally correct to assert the claim "That argument is valid." This suggests the following possible form of logical pluralism.

**Carnapian Pluralism:** It only makes sense to call a logic correct internal to a framework. The correctness of a logic flows from the constitutive rules of the framework.

For the tolerant philosopher, more than one logic is correct relative to a framework, because more than one framework can be productive for theoretical, scientific work.

If there is a weakness of Carnapian pluralism, it is its reliance on explicit stipulation and its reticence to impose any limitations. There is a grain of truth to the view that scientists can stipulate their concepts and methods of reasoning, but to a large extent the frameworks that matter in scientific discourse are just as public as natural language. The rules of the framework are not in any one person's control. Furthermore, we can imagine random combinations of rules that could never constitute a useful framework for anyone (see Section 3.3). Tolerance is so permissive that it looks like total freedom rather than constrained freedom, which is just not a very interesting view at the end of the day. We revisit such worries for logical pluralism in Section 3.2.

This brings us to Tarski's influential work on validity (or logical consequence). This work is also ripe for pluralist interpretation, but it is not quite as permissive as tolerance. We will only scratch the surface. For a more thorough treatment of this topic you may want to consult the Cambridge Element *Logical Consequence* (Sher, 2022).

Tarski (1936) codified the prominent, model-theoretic approach to logic. Recall that models in this sense are mathematical structures that assign semantic values to formulas. Tarski explicates the concept of "following logically" as follows.

> We say that the sentence $X$ follows logically from the sentences of the class $K$ if and only if every model of the class $K$ is at the same time a model of the sentence $X$. (Tarski, 2002, p. 186)

Tarski ties this explication of validity to models. $K$ is a collection of premises and $X$ is the conclusion of a given argument. In Section 1.4, we looked at various definitions of models and what it is for a model to assign a designated value to a formula. This is the same thing that Tarski calls "being a model of" that formula. So, he is stating a semantic definition of validity that looks just like definitions we still use today.

Logical properties are supposed to have a modal dimension. If the Tarskian definition works, it may demystify these properties by equating them with generalizations about models. For example, the fact that a trivial theory is impossible is equivalent to the fact that *there is no model* that makes all of its sentences true. Since models have a precise mathematical definition, the existence of certain models is perfectly clear.

The success of this method, however, requires a range of models. And variations between models (within the model theory of a single logic) rely on the distinction between logical and non-logical vocabulary. For example, in propositional logic we saw how a connective like $\wedge$ is part of the logical vocabulary, but a sentence letter like $p$ is non-logical. The evaluation policy for the connective is fixed across all models. The value assigned to a sentence letter is always a semantic value 1 or 0, but this can change between models and points of evaluation in models. All three model theories that we discuss are like this. Tarski's approach relies on models, but a precise definition of *what models are* relies on a divide between logical and non-logical vocabulary.

To the extent that Tarski has pluralist sympathies, this comes out with respect to the question of how to demarcate the logical vocabulary in a formal language. In his early work on the topic, Tarski (1936) remarks that the choice of where to demarcate the logical vocabulary "is certainly not entirely arbitrary" (p. 188 of the 2002 translation). He goes on, however, to say "I know of no objective reasons which would allow one to draw a precise dividing line between the two categories of terms." Instead of "precise" perhaps the better word would be "absolute." The list of logical vocabulary in a formal language is clear and precise, but must it be designed in just that way once and for all?

Consider a series of nested formal languages progressing from the standard language of propositional logic to that of first-order logic and second-order logic. The more complex languages recognize elements of argument form – occurrences of certain terms, predicates, and quantifiers – that are ignored or glossed over by the simpler languages. What reason could we have to view one of these systems as the absolutely correct representation of argument form? What does that even mean? In his early work, Tarski is hesitant and uncertain about this issue. He is inclined to think of formal languages as novel means of expressions and objects of study in their own right. It does seem pretty unclear why there would be stringent constraints on the demarcation of logical vocabulary in this setting. This suggests the following possible form of logical pluralism:

**Tarskian Pluralism:** There is more than one eligible way to demarcate the logical vocabulary. Each one produces a correct, model-theoretic definition of validity.

On this view, there are as many correct logics as there are eligible demarcations of logical vocabulary. Tarski suggests that this may be flexible, but not arbitrary. He was pretty firmly committed to classical logic throughout his career, so Tarski might have accepted that classical propositional logic, first-order logic, and second-order logic are each correct relative to different, eligible choices of the logical vocabulary. If there is no fact of the matter about which vocabulary must be classified "logical," then we have a plurality of logics that are as correct as any logic can be. The form of pluralism just sketched would be significantly more restrained than Carnapian pluralism.

However, Tarski (1986) later floated the idea that logical vocabulary might be identified, in some absolute sense, with expressions that are formal.

This *invariantist* approach was elaborated by Sher (1991) (see also Bonnay (2008) and Griffiths and Paseau (2022)). Loosely speaking, the idea is to take the mathematical set theory, ZFC, as a guide to understanding what counts as a formal or structural property. We consider extensional properties of sets that do not change when that set is transformed. It is plausible to call these properties "formal" and any symbol that expresses them "logical." If Tarskian invariantism is successful, it may undermine Tarskian pluralism.

It is hard to say where the real, historical Tarski fell on the question of correct logic. For one thing, the debate over logical pluralism and even the framing of such a question was not around during his lifetime. When it comes to the role of logical vocabulary in the model-theoretic approach, Tarski was simply of two minds about the demarcation question. He fluctuated between the view that this is a pragmatic choice (pluralism) and the view that there is a substantive criterion of logicality (monism).

In this section, we highlighted salient pluralist-friendly themes that originated with Carnap and Tarski. Their work is suggestive of specific, possible pluralist views on logic. Varzi (2002) refers to the claim that "the logical vocabulary is up for grabs" as Tarskian relativism and the claim that "the meaning of the logical vocabulary is up for grabs" as Carnapian relativism. These slogans have a methodological source. For these two philosophers, logic is a formal tool that we shape to our purposes. The question of what follows from what only has a determinate answer when it is addressed to a formal theory, but there is more than one good way to build such theories.

## 2.3 Idealization Pluralism

The previous section explored pluralism that arises from the design of formal systems, subject to a minimum of external constraints. Carnap and Tarski are attracted to such views because they think that everyday thought and language are not precise enough to be the subjects of logical study. Haack (1978) and Cook (2002) call this *instrumentalism* about logic because it primarily treats logics as useful tools.

Most pluralists view things a bit differently. They believe that logic does, in fact, capture some preexisting phenomenon that is part of natural language or our epistemic lives. Haack (1978) uses the terms "system-relative validity" to refer to the internal judgments of a logical system and "extra-systemic validity" to refer to the phenomenon that those systems aim to capture. This serves a similar function as Priest's notion of a canonical application: the extrasystemic phenomenon determines when a logic is correct.

Haack (1978, pp. 227–231) herself defends an early, noninstrumental version of logical pluralism. This view is predicated on an influential idea about the relationship between logics and meaning known as the *meaning-variance* thesis. This topic will come back many times and is the entire focus of Section 3.3, but for now a quick overview is fine. As Quine (1986) puts it: a change of logic constitutes a change of meaning. Think about the system-relative validities involving negation in the propositional logics in Section 1. Some of these logics validate excluded middle and others don't, some validate explosion and others don't. According to the meaning-variance thesis, these differences reflect different *theories of meaning* about negation. More generally, logics that accept different laws for a symbol attach different meanings to that symbol. The usual interpretations of proof theory and model theory reinforce this link between logic and meaning.

Haack thinks that extrasystemic validity is a feature of natural language, so logical correctness arises from the relation between logic and natural language. Logic is not an explication, but a representation. For example, the negation symbol ¬ is meant to capture properties of our real concept of negation, exemplified by the use of "not" in English. But expressions of negation in natural language have independent meaning so, by meaning-variance, logics with different laws for ¬ offer competing representations of that real meaning. It seems like only one of these representations can be correct.

This suggests that if logic is a study of linguistic phenomena, then meaning-variance quickly implies logical monism. In response, Haack points out a possibility "which has tended to be overlooked in the debate about meaning-variance."

> Formalization involves a certain abstraction from what are taken to be irrelevant or unimportant features of informal discourse; the logician feels free to ignore the temporal connotations of 'and', say, or the plurality implied by 'some'. And this leaves scope for, so to speak, alternative formal projections of the same informal discourse. (Haack, 1978, p. 230)

The general idea here is that logical tools are *idealizations* of some kind, which by nature are only imperfect representations of natural language phenomena.

Quite apart from the debate over logical pluralism, this idea has gained a lot of traction in recent years. For example, Cook (2002, 2010) argues that formal logics are intentionally inaccurate representations of natural language. The reason is that logics are like scientific models, which gain simplicity and explanatory power by abstracting away from certain details of the target phenomenon. The idealizations involved in scientific modeling aid understanding, but this goes hand-in-hand with a degree of inaccuracy. A perfect map is a poor model because it is no different from the terrain itself, which we need the map to navigate (Korzybski, 1931). Glanzberg (2015, 2021) echoes this sentiment when he argues that logics are "carefully designed controlled environments." The function of a logic is analogous to that of a model organism in biological research.

On this idealization view, logics represent natural language validity. The notion of natural language validity and the suitability of logics to study such a thing is controversial. If validity is a matter of truth-preservation, this view may require that natural language speakers grasp complex truth-conditions. Dummett (1978) argues that this would be so intractable as to make language acquisition impossible. If validity is a matter of rule-following, this view may require that natural language speakers grasp an indefinite number of rules. Kripke (1982) argues that this would make it indeterminate when two speakers mean the same thing. Some logical nihilists argue that formal logics are unsuited to the task of representing natural language validity (Cotnoir, 2018).

If those issues can be resolved for the idealization pluralist, we then want to know what makes the difference between good and bad abstraction? It probably depends on our goals. Logic in mathematics is supposed to help streamline proofs, so many facets of natural language are safely ignored for this purpose. Logic in philosophy is often deployed to clarify puzzles about knowledge and vagueness, so it has to pay attention to facets of natural language that are not important in mathematics. So, the goals of modeling are a salient parameter in the success of a given logic.

On this view, a correct logic is one that is "good enough" at representing natural language validity relative to its goals. Haack argues for roughly the following thesis by relying on such a parametric notion of correctness:

**Idealization Pluralism:** More than one logic is a correct representation of validity, in the sense that it is inaccurate but good enough relative to its goals.

Different logics can encode "different representations of the same [informal] arguments" (Haack, 1978, p. 231), even give different judgments of validity, yet they can both be correct in this sense. Cook (2002, 2010) calls this logic-as-modelling pluralism.

For a pluralist of this stripe, perhaps the most sensible thing to say is that the less consensus there is about a given logical principle, the lower our credence should be in that principle. One site of constant dispute between classical logic and a variety of non-classical logics is the principle of excluded middle. If there are logics on both sides that are correct idealizations with similarly aligned goals, this at least points toward some confounding factor in our grasp of natural language validity that makes it unclear whether or not we should really accept excluded middle. We might take the best settled view on logical laws to emerge from supervaluation over the collection of all correct logics (with similar goals). This does not convert the view into logical monism because each individual logic is still just as correct of a representation as it needs to be.

The idealization view offers a potential reply to meaning-variance. If logics imperfectly represent, then two logics with different laws may be representations of the same thing. Distinct formal treatments of negation might both be imperfect representations of the same natural language expression. If some aspects of real negation have an interesting representation in one logic and other aspects have an interesting representation in another logic, both could be correct in the parametric sense defined above.

Idealization pluralism can also live alongside certain Tarskian ideas we saw earlier. Some authors suggest reasons to see them as natural bedfellows. When we try to raise the demarcation issue in the context of natural language, there is simply no fact of the matter about the logical vocabulary (Lycan, 1989; Glanzberg, 2015). Furthermore, for an idealization pluralist, it is no problem to evaluate and compare logics across different families from a single, external point of view, as long as they are evaluated by different standards: The facets of natural language that one logic prioritizes may differ from another. We now have an abundance of reasons to accept some degree of logical pluralism based on considerations about the tools and methods of logic.

Terrés Villalonga (2019) argues for a slightly different, though related view on logic that is meant to blend elements from the semantics and pragmatics of natural language. If semantics is about the literal meanings of words, then pragmatics is about meaning that gets conveyed in conversation. You ask someone at work "Is Ann coming to lunch?" and he says "She's on holiday." You infer "No, Ann is not coming to lunch" as an answer to your original question, even though that is far from the literal meaning of his words.

Terrés Villalonga argues that classical logic and relevant logic formalize different properties of natural language connectives, some of which are pragmatically important. To illustrate the idea, consider the use of "and" in English. When a person says "I will eat dinner and go to sleep" we might understand them to mean that these events will happen in a certain order. This ordering is not part of the literal meaning of "and" but it is often part of the pragmatically conveyed information. In classical logic, $p \wedge q$ is equivalent to $q \wedge p$. In strong relevant logics, there is another kind of conjunction operator for which $p \otimes q$ is not equivalent to $q \otimes p$. The first one seems to track the literal meaning of "and" while the second one tracks certain pragmatic interpretations. According to Terrés Villalonga, these different idealizations are correct for different purposes.

Like the views in the previous section, we can see how idealization pluralism stems from methodological considerations. This kind of pluralism arises from an inherently loose representational relation between logics and natural language. However, there is a clearer standard of correctness than on the Carnapian view. Idealization pluralism, thus, promises a robust constrained freedom regarding the plurality of correct logics.

Perhaps the biggest outstanding question for this view is whether its methodological story is plausible. Is logic primarily a study of linguistic phenomena? Not all logicians accept this story, especially those like Carnap who see logic as a creative tool. There is a lot more work to be done on this approach to logic and its implications for pluralism.

## 2.4 Case-Based Pluralism

The preceding views argue that pluralism arises from a mismatch between logics and their motivating phenomena (many useful explications or imperfect representations). In the debate over logical pluralism, however, this is not the dominant theme.

A more widely discussed route to pluralism starts from the idea that our pretheoretic concept of validity suffers from a distinctive form of indeterminacy. In this section, we discuss such a view on which validity is understood in terms of truth-preservation, though this is more of a slogan than a full definition. The overall structure of this view is much like that of alethic pluralism: There is one concept realized in many ways.

Beall and Restall (2000, 2006) developed the most influential view of this kind, known as *case-based* pluralism. This view is inspired by Tarski's model-theoretic approach, but where Tarski refers to models, they refer instead to *cases*. Beall and Restall characterize the concept of validity with something called the Generalized Tarski Thesis (GTT).

**(GTT)** An argument is valid$_x$ if and only if, in every case$_x$ in which the premises are true, so is the conclusion. (Beall and Restall, 2006, p. 29)

There is a parameter $x$ for cases built into this definition. Beall and Restall (2006, p. 89) say that cases are "things in which sentences may or may not be true." This is not far off from how we think about semantic models. The difference is that models are a logician's invention for the purpose of precision and explication, whereas Beall and Restall intend for cases to be something that we already grasp pretheoretically. However, there is a fairly straightforward relation between the two notions: A semantic model basically represents the salient structural features of a case (or some set of cases).

According to the GTT, any putative account of validity goes hand-in-hand with a specification of cases. The most important driving claim in case-based pluralism is that there is more than one admissible specification of cases. When the case parameter is filled one way, the GTT outputs one correct logic (extensional definition of validity), and when it is specified in a different way, the GTT outputs another correct logic.

Philosophers talk about worlds, states of affairs, and other things in which sentences may be true. These are examples of how cases can be specified in different ways. It is not hard to understand that different accounts of cases exist, but case-based pluralism rests on the more controversial claim that different accounts of cases yield correct instances of the GTT. What does that mean? The argument for this claim is partly based on inherent features of cases (the input side of the GTT) but it is mostly driven by the features of the corresponding accounts of validity (the output side of the GTT).

Beall and Restall argue that validity is supposed to be a *necessary*, *formal*, and *normative* relation. They appeal to the core tradition in logic to support this list of features. A logic is correct if its notion of validity has all of the core features.

**Case-Based Pluralism:** More than one logic defines a relation that realizes the (GTT) concept of validity and has all of the traditional features of validity.

Beall and Restall go on to say *which logics* they think are correct, but a case-based pluralist does not have to agree on this exact list of logics. Case-based pluralism is just a view about specifications of the GTT that have all of the traditional features. Two case-based pluralists can disagree about *which logics* fall into this category.

However, for a clearer understanding of this view we can look at how Beall and Restall defend specific logics. The strategy is to compare various logical systems in a shared language. They contrast this with Carnapian pluralism: "For Carnap, plurality in logic arose because we were free to choose the kinds of languages we might use…For us, pluralism can arise *within* a language" (Beall and Restall, 2006, pp. 78–79).

The culprit lies with the criteria of necessity, formality, and normativity, which are said to be satisfiable in different ways. Beall and Restall (2006, p. 24) understand necessity as truth in all possible worlds. A logic has an appropriate tie to necessity if its underlying cases can simulate the set of possible worlds as a subset. The criterion of formality has to do with a notion of independence along the lines of Tarskian invariantism. A logic should be defined in such a way that it does not care about the specific identities of objects it is applied to. For example, suppose we have a first-order model that quantifiers over just three dogs that have the property of being friendly, expressed by $F$, and a model that quantifiers over just three cats that have the property of being fluffy, expressed by predicate $F$. The exact same formulas are true in these models. The criterion of normativity concerns evaluations of rational belief. In principle, there are numerous ways that a formal system could have some normative importance. Beall and Restall claim that logic identifies prohibitive norms of the form: Do not accept *this* (premise) and reject *that* (conclusion) because valid reasoning can lead you from one to the other. There is more than one correct logic definable by the GTT that somehow satisfies the preceding criteria.

To support this view, Beall and Restall identify three interesting conceptions of cases. They apply the GTT to each one and argue that it produces a definition that meets all of the traditional requirements of logic. On this view, because the concept of validity is indeterminate, there are just *different kinds* of validity for arguments.

One natural conception of cases to consider is that of *possible worlds*. According to Beall and Restall, classical models represent the abstract structure of possible worlds. If we input this specification of cases into the GTT, we get out the classical account of validity. Classical validity is necessary because of the correspondence between worlds and classical models: "if there is a possible world invalidating an argument, then there is some…model also invalidating that argument" (Beall and Restall, 2006, p. 40). The properties of vocabulary ascribed by classical semantics are considered formal in a technical (invariantist) sense, which we briefly mentioned in Section 2.2. And classical logic supports prohibitive norms because it is truth-preserving, hence any classically invalid argument involves a mistake of "stepping from truth to untruth." This is why classical models representing worlds are admissible cases, and classical logic is a correct logic.

Some linguists appeal to a notion of localized states of affairs or small regions of worlds also known as *situations* (Barwise and Perry, 1983; Kratzer, 2023). Situations are meant to reduce the content of attitudes. They can be incomplete: I see that a cat is on a mat in my local situation, but I don't see that it is raining on Venus or not raining on Venus. There is a truth-gap with respect to Venus facts in this situation. Situations can also be inconsistent: Ann believes that Rihanna is beautiful, she believes that Robyn Fenty is not beautiful, so her belief-situation represents one person with conflicting properties. There is a truth-glut with respect to Rihanna facts in this situation.

According to Beall and Restall, relevant models represent the abstract structure of situations. If we input them into the GTT, we get out a relevant account of validity. As we mentioned in Section 1.5, every relevant model is a generalization of some classical model, so according to Beall and Restall there is an appropriate tie between situations and possible worlds. Relevant logic does seem just as formal as other logics and, most importantly, according to Beall and Restall it supports norms that track exactly the right kind of relevance violations: Every invalid argument mistakenly draws a conclusion whose truth "does not come *from* the truth of the premises." This is when premises are irrelevant to a given conclusion, which is a source of logical mistakes distinct from those associated with classical logic. This is why relevant models representing situations are admissible cases, and relevant logic is a correct logic.

In Section 1, we discussed several ways in which intuitionistic philosophy motivates a notion of *constructive stages*. Beall and Restall (2006, p. 68) contend that such stages are incomplete and yet "*totally specified* (disjunctions are not left dangling without witnessing disjuncts, and existential quantifications also have witnesses)." They claim that model theory for intuitionistic logic represents the abstract structure of stages. If we input this notion into the GTT, we get out eactly the intuitionistic account of validity. As we mentioned in Section 1.5, every intuitionistic model is a generalization of some classical model, so according to Beall and Restall there is an appropriate tie between stages and possible worlds. Intuitionistic logic seems just as formal as any other logic and, most importantly, according to Beall and Restall it supports important norms: every invalid argument mistakenly draws a conclusion that "goes *beyond* what it said in the premises." This is when premises fail to warrant a given conclusion, which is a source of logical mistakes distinct from those associated with classical logic. This is why intuitionistic models representing stages are admissible cases, and intuitionistic logic is a correct logic.

To appreciate the repercussions of this view, recall that the following argument violates relevance considerations (see Section 1.5). For Beall and Restall, this means that there are two answers to the question of whether this argument makes a logical mistake.

---

**Example 10**

(10.1) Dolphins are smart.
∴ If the sky is blue, then dolphins are smart.

## Logical Pluralism

This argument is valid in one way (classically), so it avoids the kind of logical mistake that corresponds with classical standards of reasoning (it does not infer falsity from truth). This argument is invalid in a different way (relevantly), so it does commit a mistake that corresponds with relevant standards (it infers the conclusion from irrelevant premises). Since these are two instances of GTT that track different kinds of mistakes, it is clear how the very same argument can be valid in one way and avoid one kind of mistake, but also be invalid in a different way and commit a different kind of mistake. These are different *logical* properties because they arise from realizations of the concept of validity.

Case-based pluralism is definitely constrained freedom. In fact, when we look at the broad array of logics out there in the literature, some of them are automatically ruled out by the GTT itself. Any instance of the GTT is a *closure* relation: a monotonic, transitive, and reflexive relation between formulas (see Humberstone (2011, ch.1) for details). This disqualifies nonmonotonic logics for defeasible reasoning Rescher and Manor (1970), linear logics for resource-bound computation Girard (1987), and nontransitive logics for dealing with paradoxes (Ripley, 2012). The definition of relevant validity from Section 1 is also disqualified by the GTT because it is nonmonotonic (recall that $p, q \nvDash_{RL} p$) much like the approach of Read (1988). (Beall and Restall semantically define relevant validity more like how we defined intuitionistic validity, simply looking at truth-preservation in all cases rather than over information chains of cases.)

One important point about case-based pluralism and some other pluralist views is that they involve an *ahistorical* interpretation of logics. Not all intuitionists or relevant logicians would accept a semantic definition of validity involving stages or states/situations. For the case-based pluralist, this does not really matter. What matters is that those logics can be interpreted in line with the GTT. This is not a criticism, just a point of clarification about the kind of philosophical theory involved with this version of pluralism.

An obvious question for the case-based pluralist is whether it is possible to define the set of absolutely all cases, leading to an all-encompassing logic. Beall and Restall (2006, p. 92) claim that there would be no reason to view such a logic as more correct than any other logic. That is one way to resist pressure toward logical monism. An even stronger reply to the challenge might run as follows. The case-based pluralist might argue that "case" is like "thing": it cannot be defined in general and can always be extended in new ways. Hence, a correct logic is always defined over a restricted set of cases that is (partly) disjoint from other sets of cases. The all-encompassing logic is a fiction.

## 2.5 Proof-Theoretic Pluralism

Case-based pluralism says that the concept of validity (truth-preservation) exhibits an interesting kind of indeterminacy. This view is tied up with the method of semantic models. We turn next to *proof-theoretic* pluralism, which says that the concept of *proof* exhibits similar indeterminacy. Unsurprisingly, this is tied up with proof rules.

We mentioned inferentialism in Section 1.3. This is the view that meaning is determined by rules of inference. We mentioned meaning-variance in Section 2.3. This is the claim that logics with different laws involving the same symbol attach different meanings to that symbol. The proof-theoretic pluralist leverages inferentialism to offer a forceful refutation of the meaning-variance thesis. According to this version of pluralism, more than one correct logic shares the same meaning-determining rules.

We will need more details in order to understand how these claims are even remotely plausible, but the overall aim is to support strong *meaning-invariance*. In the discussion of idealization pluralism, we mentioned one way to defend the idea of a shared meaning across logics with different laws. However, this is only because those logics are intended as imperfect representations in the first place. There is looseness between the logic and the meaning it represents. Proof-theoretic pluralism advocates for a much stronger claim: Logics involving different laws for the same symbol can attach exactly the same meaning to that symbol. How is that possible?

In order to explain this, we need to visit the *sequent calculus*, a style of proof theory that is somewhat different from Hilbert systems (see Section 1.3). A sequent is a structure of formulas that generalizes on the notion of an argument. We will use large greek letters like $\Gamma, \Delta$ to refer to sets of formulas. A sequent has two sides with sets of formulas occurring on either side and a separator between them like this: $\Gamma, p \Rightarrow q, \Delta$. Typical arguments have a single conclusion, but note that a sequent may have multiple formulas on its right side. We interpret this through the lens of speech act theory (Restall, 2005).

Agents can assert things and deny things. We call a combination of speech acts a position. Some positions are *incoherent*. The clearest example is when an agent asserts and denies the very same thing. We can build up a definition of derivations *between* entire sequent structures using proof rules that *preserve* incoherence. If a sequent $\Gamma \Rightarrow \Delta$ is derivable, that means it is incoherent to assert all of the $\Gamma$s and deny all of the $\Delta$s.

The starting point is any sequent with the form $p \Rightarrow p$. This is called an *initial* sequent and it encodes the most basic instance of positional incoherence. As we said earlier, it is obviously incoherent to assert and deny the same thing. That is what initial sequents represent. We try to build up other derivable sequents from these initial sequents.

For that, we need some rules. Each rule is written in a stack, with sequents on top and bottom. If the top sequent is derivable (captures a limitation on coherence), then the bottom sequent is also derivable (captures a limitation on coherence). Some rules manipulate the structure of sequents, like the *weakening* rules:

$$\frac{\Gamma \Rightarrow \Delta}{\Sigma, \Gamma \Rightarrow \Delta} \text{[WL]} \qquad \frac{\Gamma \Rightarrow \Delta}{\Gamma \Rightarrow \Delta, \Sigma} \text{[WR]}$$

On our interpretation, for example, the rule WL says: if it is incoherent to assert the $\Gamma$s and deny the $\Delta$s, it is also incoherent to assert the $\Sigma$s and $\Gamma$s and deny the $\Delta$s. This makes sense since the addition of more assertions cannot remove incoherence.

Other types of sequent rules are more specific. They only apply to sequents with specific operators in them. Here is an example of the proof rules for negation:

$$\frac{\Gamma \Rightarrow p, \Delta}{\Gamma, \neg p \Rightarrow \Delta} \text{[}\neg\text{L]} \qquad \frac{\Gamma, p \Rightarrow \Delta}{\Gamma \Rightarrow \neg p, \Delta} \text{[}\neg\text{R]}$$

On our interpretation, for example, the rule $\neg L$ says something like this: if it is incoherent to deny $p$ in a certain context, it is also incoherent to assert $\neg p$ in that same context (thinking of the asserted $\Gamma$s and denied $\Delta$s as the surrounding context). This captures the idea that the function of negation is to communicate denial.

Here are the rules for conjunction:

$$\frac{\Gamma, p_i \Rightarrow \Delta}{\Gamma, p_1 \wedge p_2 \Rightarrow \Delta} \text{[}\wedge\text{L]} \qquad \frac{\Gamma \Rightarrow p, \Delta \quad \Gamma \Rightarrow q, \Delta}{\Gamma \Rightarrow p \wedge q, \Delta} \text{[}\wedge\text{R]}$$

Using the rule $\wedge L$, if it is incoherent to assert $p_1$, then it is incoherent to assert $p_1 \wedge p_2$. Likewise, if it is incoherent to assert $p_2$, then it is incoherent to assert $p_1 \wedge p_2$. Both inferences are permitted. Using the $\wedge R$ rule, if we know separately that it is incoherent to deny $p$ and incoherent to deny $q$, then it is incoherent to deny $p \wedge q$.

Here are the rules for disjunction:

$$\frac{\Gamma, p \Rightarrow \Delta \quad \Gamma, q \Rightarrow \Delta}{\Gamma, p \vee q \Rightarrow \Delta} [\vee L] \qquad \frac{\Gamma \Rightarrow p_i, \Delta}{\Gamma \Rightarrow p_1 \vee p_2, \Delta} [\vee R]$$

They have a dual reading to the conjunction rules.

For a complete sequent calculus, we need rules for each logical operator and a variety of structural rules. Once we have all of these rules, we can build derivations. A derivation looks like a tree narrowing down toward its root. The very top starting points are initial sequents of the form $p \Rightarrow p$. Each step moving down the tree is licensed by one of the proof rules. Any sequent that comes out at the end of this procedure, in the root of such a tree, is a *derivable sequent* that represents a valid argument form.

For example, here are classical derivations of explosion and excluded middle:

$$\frac{\dfrac{\dfrac{\dfrac{\dfrac{p \Rightarrow p}{p \Rightarrow p, q}[WR]}{p, \neg p \Rightarrow q}[\neg L]}{(p \wedge \neg p), \neg p \Rightarrow q}[\wedge L]}{(p \wedge \neg p), (p \wedge \neg p) \Rightarrow q}[\wedge L]}{(p \wedge \neg p) \Rightarrow q}[CL]$$

$$\frac{\dfrac{\dfrac{\dfrac{\dfrac{p \Rightarrow p}{q, p \Rightarrow p}[WL]}{q \Rightarrow p, \neg p}[\neg R]}{q \Rightarrow (p \vee \neg p), \neg p}[\vee R]}{q \Rightarrow (p \vee \neg p), (p \vee \neg p)}[\vee R]}{q \Rightarrow (p \vee \neg p)}[CR]$$

The derivation of explosion *requires* putting multiple formulas on the left side in some intermediate steps, and the derivation of excluded middle *requires* putting multiple formulas on the right side in some intermediate steps.

Let's use $R$ to refer to the sequent rules for classical logic. Gentzen (1969) showed that if we *only* allow sequents with single conclusions to appear in intermediate steps, then the same rules $R$ define intuitionistic validity. The derivation of excluded middle is impossible in this system because it uses $\neg R$ to collect the denial of $p$ and $\neg p$ together on the right side. Restall (2014) points out that if we *only* allow sequents with single premises to appear in intermediate steps, then the same rules $R$ actually define a paraconsistent notion of validity (this is called dual-intuitionistic logic and it is somewhat different from the relevant/paraconsistent logics we discussed earlier). The derivation of explosion is impossible in this system because it uses $\neg L$ to collect the assertion of $p$ and $\neg p$ together on the left side. So, we have three logics from one set of rules.

In these logics, we have rules and policies that, when put together, produce an extensional definition of proofs. Gentzen and Restall show how to vary the extensional definition of proofs without varying the underlying rules. If we think that certain rules are essential to proofs, then a logic can be called correct as long as it is defined from those rules. Restall advocates this version of the pluralist thesis.

**Proof-Theoretic Pluralism:** More than one logic (defined in this sequent calculus) is a correct definition of proofs, or rule-governed valid argument forms.

A crucial, implicit assumption of this view is that rules that are essential to the concept of proof do not include specific policies about how many premises or conclusions are allowed. This creates some flexibility and, thus, indeterminacy in the concept of proof that allows for different realizations. On this view, because the concept of proof is indeterminate, there are genuinely *different kinds* of proofs.

Ole Hjortland (2013) points out another result of this kind, which involves an even more complex proof theory with three-sided sequents. In this setting, he shows that we can define classical logic as well as the three-valued logics K3 and LP from the same rules. Dicher (2020) and Ferrari and Orlandelli (2021) offer yet more related results. The details are quite different between some of these theories, but the overall picture is similar: they identify a set of essential rules, then they show how to vary the extensional definition of proofs without varying the underlying rules. On this approach to pluralism, we can vary all kinds of policies about building derivations. As long as we do not touch the underlying rules, we do not change the concept of proof captured in such a logic.

There are two pressing issues for proof-theoretic pluralism. First, what is the target concept of proof? What can be said about our pre-theoretic grasp of this concept before we start to pin it down formally? Can the pluralist offer a simple, condensed characterization of her rule-following conception of validity akin to the GTT? This would help to flesh out the repercussions of her view. Presumably proof-theoretic pluralists are not trying to describe everyday reasoning. The "incoherence" reading of sequents suggests that the notion captured by the sequent calculus represents standards of reasoning that are too complicated for agents to follow in ordinary conversation.

Second, and somewhat related, why are the logics defined from the rules above all *correct* logics? The greatest achievement of this approach to logical pluralism is that it offers a truly compelling and precise notion of meaning that can be shared across logics. However, this only solves the aim of reconciling distinct logics. It allows for a plurality of logics, but it does not yet explain why the extensional definitions of validity that flow from *those* rules in particular are correct definitions of validity (see also Kouri (2016)). An account of the pretheoretic concept of proof formalized by this set of rules would go a long way toward supporting this claim. We revisit this issue in Section 3.3 where we focus entirely on how meaning-variance interacts with the project of logical pluralism.

## 2.6 Eclectic Pluralism

Another strain of pluralism, also known as *eclecticism*, deserves some attention due to its distinctive argument strategy. Most pluralists appeal to features of logical methods or concepts in order to explain why there is not just one uniquely correct logic. They rarely offer nonphilosophical evidence. It is not easy to imagine what that would look like. Shapiro (2011, 2014a,b) attempts to offer such evidence. He sets the tone with the question: "Is there more than one logic that is employed – or can be employed, or should be employed – in legitimate mathematical theories?" (Shapiro, 2014b, p.1).

This question is intentionally narrow. Shapiro wants to keep our focus entirely on mathematical practice. Why do so? One interesting reason is that this may strengthen the evidential basis of our philosophical views on logic. If we rely on natural language and every reasoning, it becomes extraordinarily difficult to isolate evidence for valid argumentation. This is much more overt in mathematics, where validity is the only thing that counts toward knowledge, hence there is a direct path from the successful proof strategies of mathematicians to an understanding of validity. This is an instance of the broadly anthropological stance known as *practice-based* philosophy of mathematics and logic (cf. Martin and Hjortland (2021)). By reflecting on legitimate mathematical theories, Shapiro argues that a logical monism is unpalatable.

Mainstream, classical mathematics takes classical logic as its standard, but there are alternatives to this tradition. The most mature alternative practice is that of constructive mathematics, which takes intuitionistic logic as its standard. Practitioners working in these traditions accept different kinds of proofs. It is not obvious that the practices cannot hang together. A hypothetical classical monist might explain the diversity of mathematical practices in the following way. Everything that is valid in intuitionistic logic is valid in classical logic. The restrictions of constructive mathematics are just a choice. The constructive mathematician avoids indirect proofs, but it does not follow that she is *correct* to do so nor that such arguments are *genuinely* invalid. From this hypothetical point of view, constructivists simply restrain themselves from using valid proof strategies. They don't have to do this. If this is true, then classical monism is saved.

# Logical Pluralism

We need more than just a diversity of practices to support interesting philosophical views about pluralism in logic. Shapiro argues from the basis of Hilbertian structuralism. This is the view that mathematics is the study of *structure*: abstract positions and relations, not specific objects. Legitimate mathematical theories describe structures. According to Hilbert (the namesake of Hilbert systems, see Section 1.3), the only thing that systemically undermines a mathematical theory is logical triviality. For the Hilbertian structuralist, any non-trivial piece of mathematics is an apt subject for further study. This is a liberal and plenitudinous view on the extent of mathematical structure.

The second important point is that, as a matter of fact, some parts of constructive mathematics are incompatible with classical standards of validity. A nice example is the theory of Smooth Infinitesimal Analysis (SIA). SIA posits infinitely small quantities that are clustered arbitrarily close to zero. These are defined indirectly. A *nilsquare* infinitesimal is defined as any quantity $\varepsilon$ such that $\varepsilon^2 = 0$. Even in classical analysis, this definition makes sense, but there is just one quantity that satisfies the definition: zero itself.

According to SIA, on the other hand, we get the result that not all nilsquares are identical with zero, but they are all *definitely nondistinct* from zero. Hellman (2006) argues that they are treated as merely potential entities with inherently vague identity conditions. As a result, it is a theorem of SIA that not every quantity is definitely identical or distinct from 0. The identity relation is generally indeterminate.

**(Theorem)** $\quad \neg \forall x(x = 0 \vee (x \neq 0))$

The theory is still non-trivial precisely because it uses intuitionistic logic. In particular, consider the following statement. This would be a disaster even for an intuitionist because it says that we can construct a specific quantity that has contradictory properties, being both distinct from 0 and nondistinct from 0.

**(Nontheorem)** $\quad \exists x((x \neq 0) \wedge \neg(x \neq 0))$

However, that disastrous implication does not follow. It is not a theorem of SIA because of the DeMorgan principle that fails in intuitionistic logic (see Section 1.5).

Nonetheless, it is important to note that if we applied fully classical reasoning to this theory, then the nontheorem would follow and outright triviality would ensue. If we deploy the full strength of classical proof strategies, we cannot even work with this theory. There are other examples of this kind, but SIA illustrates the point that the relationship between classical and constructive mathematics is more complex than envisioned by the hypothetical logical monist we described earlier. Specifically, these contraclassical theories exhibit aspects of constructive practice that are not *optional restrictions*.

If mainstream mathematics witnesses the epistemic utility of (fully) classical proof strategies, then SIA provides evidence of their limitations. And for the Hilbertian, there is no reason to wonder if such theories are legitimate: "[W]e have an interesting field with the look and feel of mathematics. It has attracted the attention of mainstream mathematicians…smooth infinitesimal analysis should count as mathematics, despite its reliance on intuitionistic logic" (Shapiro, 2014b, p. 75). Thus, we have a kind of *mathematical pluralism* in the first instance. On the structuralist mathematical pluralist picture, each structure occupies its own corner of the mathematical universe, but the logical texture differs from one structure to another.

This mathematical pluralism can then support an argument for logical pluralism. We saw that SIA is trivial according to the classical definition of triviality. The idea that constructive restrictions are a choice does nothing to explain how *this* kind of theory can be accepted from a classical point of view. In order to respect contraclassical theories as legitimate parts of mathematics, we have to acknowledge that the legitimizing property of non-triviality cannot always be understood as *classical* non-triviality. SIA is trivial by classical standards, yet still legitimate in a different way. Shapiro (2014b, p. 67) says, "[T]he crucial, if trite, observation is that consistency is a matter of logic.…the weaker the logic, the more theories that are consistent, and thus legitimate from the Hilbertian perspective." We have the following version of logical pluralism:

**Eclectic Pluralism:** More than one logic realizes the concepts of validity and triviality that are salient to mathematical truth and ontology.

This argument for pluralism is "not primarily deductive…It is more like an inference to the best explanation." Logical pluralism enters in as an explanatory hypothesis because it offers us the simplest prediction of a diversity of reasoning practices and a range of theories that are non-trivial in different ways (as observed).

Caret (2021) reconstructs this explanatory argument as follows:

- Assumption: Legitimacy requires non-triviality.
- Observation: We see from mathematical practice that there are legitimate theories that cannot be accommodated by mainstream, classical mathematics.
- Explanation: There is more than one kind of non-triviality.

The success of this line of thought is contested. Priest (2021) argues that the eclectic argument is wrong because mathematical pluralism does not require logical pluralism. There is certainly more to think about regarding the evidence from mathematical practice.

Kouri Kissel and Shapiro (2020) call the eclectic view a form of domain-relative pluralism, meaning that (at least in mathematics) the *structure* about which we want to prove things determines the correct logical standard for our proofs. Each mathematical structure constitutes a different subject matter. The question of logical correctness only has a determinate answer relative to such a subject matter. This shows that the eclectic view gives up on one of the traditional aspirations of logic: a *universal* canon of reasoning. We come back to this theme in several places in Section 3.

It might seem like this view should have broad implications as well: if logical pluralism holds in mathematics it should hold more generally. Shapiro seems to shy away from such claims because he wants to stick closely to the evidence from practice, and this evidence is only clear in the setting of mathematics. Taken to an extreme, this could amount to skepticism about logical properties in natural language – that there *are any* to study, or that they are *precise enough* to support interesting logical theory. In this respect, we find echoes of both Carnap and Tarski in the eclectic pluralist view.

## 2.7 Looking Around

Pluralistic perspectives on logic are wide-ranging and varied. Maybe this is no surprise. Logical pluralists are interested in a variety of issues: logical vocabulary, idealized models of natural language, indeterminate logical concepts, and regimented reasoning practices. Pluralists accept criteria of logical correctness that are permissive enough to be satisfied by many distinct logics, even logics that were traditionally taken to be incompatible rivals. This may even *reconcile* some disagreements about logic.

Several issues are worth further comment. For one, there is the issue of truth and truth-bearers. These are important to logic and may be additional sources of pluralism. For another thing, there are lingering questions about relativization. In this section, we will visit some of those additional corners of the pluralist literature.

We mentioned truth pluralism once before as a nice example of pluralistic philosophy with some affinities to logical pluralism. Pedersen (2014) argues for a tight connection between these two doctrines: he argues that truth pluralism implies logical pluralism. Think of *correspondence with facts* as a property that realizes truth for statements in one discourse domain, and *warrant to believe* as a property that realizes truth in another domain. On this view, the question of which arguments are truth-preserving needs to be refined: do we mean the correspondence property or the warrant property? This is another way in which validity (truth-preservation) may be parameterized. Pedersen argues that these have logically relevant structural differences. In domains where the correspondence property applies, either $p$ corresponds to the facts or $\neg p$ corresponds to the facts. With respect to this property, excluded middle holds. However, in domains where the warrant property applies, it can occur that neither $p$ nor $\neg p$ is warranted. With respect to this property, excluded middle fails. Different domains yield different logics.

Domains have come up in two ways so far. The ecclectic pluralist identifies them with mathematical structures, while the truth pluralist *à la* Pedersen treats them more thematically (value judgments, perceptual reports, etc.). Bueno and Shalkowski (2009) defend another domain-relative pluralist view based on *modalism*: the view that modal concepts are irreducible primitives (Shalkowski, 1994). Bueno and Shalkowski argue that different, primitive notions of possibility are triggered by reasoning about different subject matters. Since logical concepts have a modal aspect, different types of modality lead to different realizations of the logical concept of triviality. What are these different types of modality? They mention two kinds. There is a type of modality that is oriented toward objective reality. In this sense, there *cannot* be a contradiction (in the world). There is another type of modality that is oriented more toward subjective attitudes. In this sense, there *can* be a contradiction (in a belief set). Bueno and Shalkowski are quite explicit on this point: "[I]t is perfectly obvious that contradictions are possible. Note: possible, not possibly true. In fact, we are all quite familiar with the fact that contradictions abound.…Philosophical works, student essays, political speeches,…[can] contain contradictions." (Bueno and Shalkowski, 2009, p. 309). The suggestion is that two different types of logical standards apply to the same theory. An inconsistent theory is trivial in one sense of the term "impossible," but the same theory is non-trivial in another sense of the term "impossible." These differences correspond with at least two different correct logics: classical logic and some kind of paraconsistent logic.

Russell (2008) argues for yet another version of logical pluralism from considerations about the *logic of demonstratives* (Kaplan, 1979, 1989). This is a logical system for reasoning with words like "I," "here," and "now." We grasp the meaning of these words at some level without knowing their reference because the reference changes from one context to another: when Ann asserts "I am hungry" the word "I" refers to her and when Bob asserts "I am hungry" the word "I" refers to him. The fixed meaning or *character* determines the *content* in each context. In any context of use, the character of the word "I" is a function that outputs the person speaking as its current content. So, a bit loosely, we can say that the character of the sentence "I am hungry" makes it express the proposition *that the speaker is hungry*. This proposition is about a different person in each context.

In this system, we can evaluate the same argument at the level of characters or contents. To see why this matters, consider the following example. Suppose that Ann is recording her thoughts in her diary and she writes down the following argument:

> **Example 11**
> (11.1) I am writing.
> ∴ Ann is writing.

In this context, both sentences express the proposition *that Ann is writing*. If we evaluate the argument with a focus on content, then the argument is valid: the content of the premise and conclusion is the same proposition, so if the premise is true the conclusion must be true. However, if we move to the characters of sentences, then we have to think about how things shake out in different contexts. Consider a context where Bob writes down this argument: the premise is still true, but the conclusion is false. If we evaluate the argument with a focus on character, then the argument is invalid. Russell (2008, p. 609) claims "[T]here is a single argument…[but] the question of its validity depends on the depth of the interpretation intended." This has some similarity to Tarskian pluralism: Both claim that a single argument can be fruitfully evaluated relative to different interpretative choices (logical vocabulary or truth-bearers).

A conversational context is an *informational* environment that provides information not only about speakers but also about their shared assumptions. One popular idea in the pluralist literature is that context may explain how parameters of logical correctness are settled (the specification of cases, incidental proof structure, discourse domain, etc.; see Hjortland, 2013; Shapiro, 2014b; Caret, 2017; Kouri Kissel, 2018; Antonsen, 2025). Why do pluralists find this attractive? This is partly because intuitions of incompatibility persist in various ways. Some pluralists are worried about unqualified endorsements of logics from different logical families. On the other hand, there are forms of qualification or relativization that they also find objectionable. We elaborate on this in the next section, but the point for now is that context may be a palatable source of parameterization.

Caret (2017) proposes a contextualist version of case-based pluralism. He draws on the following idea from epistemic contextualism: when agents in different contexts are concerned with different sets of epistemic possibilities, this shifts the standard for knowledge (Cohen, 1988; DeRose, 1992; Lewis, 1996). Caret develops an analogous view about logic: when agents in different contexts are concerned with different sets of cases, this shifts the (GTT) standard for logical correctness. For eclectic pluralists, a mathematical structure *qua* discourse domain is settled by the context of mathematical practice.

On these contextualist views, we should say that a logic is only correct or incorrect in specific contexts. These views need to explain how the salient parameters are settled, especially when those parameters are complex and abstract entities.

Kouri Kissel (2021) uses context to handle lingering worries about meaning for the eclectic pluralist. If classical and constructive arithmetic have different logics, do they really share the same meaning of "number"? Are they different flavors of one thing, *arithmetic*? Is there an intertheoretic context with enough shared assumption that these theorists can univocally communicate? Kouri Kissell argues that this is resolved by mathematicians themselves through a process of metalinguistic negotation. In essence, the theorems in different theories are interpreted to have *the same* meaning in some negotiated contexts, but interpreted to have *different* meanings in other negotiated contexts. The question of real meaning is like a Carnapian illegitimate question without any answer. We will bring this back in the next section, when we consider the general challenge of accounting for shared meaning between different logics.

We see that pluralists are divided over certain issues. One is the issue of reductivism. Tarskian pluralists and case-based pluralists favor reductive definitions, while modalists and eclectic pluralists typically reject them. There is another divide over the question of whether the content of logical theory is primarily descriptive or normative. Pluralists who emphasize the semantic study of truth-preservation often see logic as descriptive, while those who emphasize proofs (good reasoning) often see logic as normative.

When we speak of normativity in connection with logic, we have in mind broadly epistemic norms pertaining to belief-regulation (Steinberger, 2019a). On many pluralist views, logic is supposed to underwrite norms of belief (or perhaps credence). Some pluralists treat this normative role as a criterion of correctness for logics. Critics argue that this underpins a normative collapse problem, which seriously threatens the internal stability of such pluralist views. We visit that topic in the next section.

A very radical view about normativity would not only assert that logic has a normative dimension, but that it is essentially normative. Hartry Field (2009, 2015) defends a view in this vicinity that allows for a version of logical pluralism with limited scope. In general, Field is an antirealist and expressivist about epistemic norms. Roughly, this means that any statement about good reasoning is just a vehicle for expressing a *nonfactual* attitude toward potential reasoning practices. Different agents have different rankings of norms that depend on their goals, experiences, and the foreseeable trade-offs of adhering to a norm. Field has complex reasons for believing that the concept of logical validity cannot be characterized in terms of *truth-preservation* (this sets Field apart and makes his view somewhat of an outlier in the literature, but nonetheless a very interesting view). Field argues that we should view the content of logical theory as specialized statements about good reasoning. When an agent asserts that an argument is valid, this is just a vehicle for expressing her intent to *draw inferences in that way*. A logic is always someone's logic.

It certainly seems like the expressivist view should admit different agent-relative logics, but according to Field, this space is quite narrow. Part of the reason is that this plurality should arise from agent-relative assessment. We need logics that could be ranked equally by the same agent with certain goals. Another reason is that logical systems are always chosen, in part, to serve the goal of providing theorems (tautologies) that are *really true*. This implies, for example, that logics with different judgments about excluded middle cannot be ranked equally. So, this kind of pluralism is much less permissive than views we have discussed throughout most of this section. Nonetheless, Field suggests tentatively that there may be the possibility of pluralism when alternative logics disagree over rules of inference and not about provable formulas.

In the last section of this Element, we will look at criticisms of logical pluralism and how pluralists may reply to them. Is logical pluralism a robust and interesting philosophical thesis? Taking into account the motivating factors for logical pluralism, can a logical monist give a better account at the end of the day? Are there problems inherent to pluralism that undermine the view? We turn to such questions next.

## 3 Challenges

### 3.1 Against Pluralism

We know what logical pluralism is about. It is time to reflect on potential challenges for this view. Critics have posed a wide array of problems, some more serious than others. Much of the critical literature focuses on case-based pluralism, but at least some of the problems raised for that view extend to other versions of logical pluralism. We will discuss three types of challenges, starting with a deceptively simple question: is logical pluralism a philosophically robust thesis? Many critics suggest that logical pluralism lacks an important degree of substance or clarity, but why do they say this?

### 3.2 Robustness

A number of critics have voiced the concern that logical pluralism may be too easy or uninteresting (Field, 2009; Eklund, 2020; Caret, 2021). These are two sides of the same coin. Williamson (2014, p. 228) says glibly, "As with so many other terms in philosophy, we may have to choose between using 'logical pluralism' to denote a boring truth and using it to denote an exciting falsehood." Why a boring truth? Consider the Tarskian pluralist who says that classical propositional logic correctly captures the arguments that are valid *merely* because of the placement of connectives, whereas first-order logic captures those and more, that is, it also captures arguments that are valid because of the placement of first-order quantifiers. Almost no one disagrees with *that* amount of pluralism.

Williamson offers other examples. Modal logics have both "local" and "global" definitions of validity. These automatically emerge from the semantic models of modal logic. They are different properties of the exact same models, so at least on the level of formal logic it is hard to find any reason to accept one of these definitions without the other. On the topic of first-order logic versus second-order logic, since "there is no sound and complete formal system of second-order logic," Williamson (2014, p. 227) says, "we may apply the word 'correct' to any of the many sound (but incomplete) formal systems of second-order logic." These claims may be taken as true, but uninteresting versions of pluralism. Williamson is right about all of this, but it does not tell us much about the versions of logical pluralism that are taken seriously in the literature.

Field (2009, pp. 345–346) remarks that it is "obviously uninteresting" to just say "that 'implies' can mean different things," although it is more exciting if we say that these are "meanings of a common type." He goes on, however, to say "I'm not sure that it's exciting *enough*." These critical remarks target case-based pluralism, but they equally apply to other views based on conceptual indeterminacy such as modalist pluralism or truth-bearer pluralism. The complaint seems to be that it is not sufficiently interesting to point out a source of conceptual indeterminacy without further commentary. Why does that indeterminacy matter? In particular, Field wants pluralism to help reconcile disagreements about logic and he is skeptical that an indeterminacy view does this.

A frequent line of criticism insists that logical pluralists are not clear enough about technical details (Goddu, 2002; Wyatt, 2004; Bremer, 2014; Keefe, 2014). There is almost certainly a grain of truth behind this complaint. When it comes to important terms like "model" and "case," it is pointless to try to define these terms in a way that is perfectly clear, but at the same time avoids any theory-laden assumptions. Nonetheless, we might expect a mature version of pluralism to flesh out these notions perhaps through a connection to metaphysics, epistemology, or philosophy of science.

Caret (2017) and Ferrari and Moruzzi (2020) point out a related worry about the way logical pluralist talks about indeterminacy. This way of speaking may unintentionally suggest that the alleged pluralist phenomena in logic bear an interesting similarity to vagueness, which is not the best way to think about this form of indeterminacy. The extension of "red" is vague. There are fuzzy, borderline cases of redness. We struggle to classify a particular sunset as being red or orange. There may be no fact of the matter. However, no one infers pluralism about redness from this sort of everyday, familiar vagueness. Admissible extensions of "red" do not seem to result from specifications of a hidden parameter in our pretheoretic concept of redness.

Logical pluralism could benefit from greater clarity about its methods. For example, do idealization pluralists have anything helpful to tell us about the nature of natural language and why we can only study it through imperfect, idealized models? Advocates of this view offer fairly thin arguments. More information would certainly be welcome.

Still, it is important to notice that the foregoing claims do not amount to rebuttals of logical pluralism. The charge that logical pluralism is "too easy" implies that some reading of the pluralist thesis is true. If we keep our attention fixed on whether the view is true, then so far we have not encountered any knock-down arguments against logical pluralism. We may want the pluralist to clarify her arguments or the repercussions of her view, but the same demands can be lodged against most philosophical projects.

However, there are deeper worries in this vicinity. Consider some of the features we associated with validity, such as its necessity and formality. The idea that these are distinctive features of validity plays an important part in the framework of case-based, modalist, and proof-theoretic logical pluralism. But are these features really topic fixing? Can we find precedent in the philosophical or mathematical tradition to vindicate a substantive set of features that distinguish validity from everything else? Griffiths (2013) and Shapiro (2014b) reject this. They claim that there is simply no consensus. In the long history of logic, conceptions of validity have shifted over time. Historic sources disagree over features such as the necessity, formality, normativity, compactness, axiomatizability, and existential commitments of logic. Shapiro even says that "flexibility concerning the nature of logic" is one of the motives for his eclectic version of pluralism.

Admittedly, this is a bit concerning. We said many times that logic is the study of validity, as if this orients our discussion toward one clear target. The historical evidence suggests that even amongst theorists, we do not have widespread agreement on the nature of that target. If monism and pluralism are supposed to be views about validity, do we even know what this debate is about? Does it have robust content?

One way to mediate this problem is to be up front about it and to appeal to something like Carnapian explication. A pluralist may acknowledge a historic lack of consensus, but say that they have reason to emphasize certain themes. Perhaps validity is a cluster concept, with formality as just one strand in the cluster. Rather than study the whole messy cluster, it may be more productive to focus on one interesting strand. There may be justification for this. For example, one might argue that a *formal* relationship promises to have unique *epistemic* value, which makes it important (compare Sher 1991). A pluralist view that is self-consciously developed along these lines cannot be accused of relying on unfounded claims of historical precedent or intuitiveness.

Is there enough *plurality* in logical pluralism? Stei (2020a) says that "Logical pluralism is a controversial view only if it can make sense of the potential rivalry between the logics." The pluralist must explain how advocates of different logics can disagree. Stei explores a reply to this challenge that accomplishes too much. Disagreements in belief consist in incompatible contents (MacFarlane (2014)'s "simple view"). Suppose we accept that "valid" is a *nonindexical* context-sensitive expression. The claim "classical laws are valid" can then be true relative to Ann's context and false relative to Bob's context. The claim "paraconsistent laws are valid" can then be true relative to Bob's context and false relative to Ann's context. Suppose these claims really cannot be true in the same context. The problem with such a view is that it abandons the essence of pluralism. We have a plurality of *true validity claims*, not a plurality of ways of being valid. In fact, these claims express the same content (nonindexicalism), so it is not the simple disagreement we wanted. There is much more to say about the topics of rivalry and disagreement, but Stei raises important questions that pluralists need to think through.

One final point of contention concerns the issue of *relativism*. Pluralists are quite divided on this label. Beall and Restall (2006, p. 88) dislike it: "We do not take logical consequence to be relative to languages, communities of inquiry, contexts, or anything else....This is a pluralism, not a relativism." On the other hand, Shapiro (2014a) embraces what he calls folk-relativity or what we have called parameterization throughout this Element. If advocates of pluralism are not even on the same page about whether they are relativists, it does raise the worry that "pluralism" is a badly defined term.

Fortunately, that's not really what is going on. This is one area where the rhetoric is misleading. Shapiro is right that all versions of pluralism are relativistic in some sense, but that's not what bothers Beall and Restall. They are concerned about a specific, overt form of relativization that they find objectionable given their understanding of our logical concepts. The objectionable kind of relativization would involve subjective phenomena like the preferences of agents. In fact, these factors do play a role in Carnapian pluralism and Field's expressivist pluralism. On those views, the claim that logic $L$ is correct is equivalent to the overtly relativized claim that $L$ satisfies some subjective parameter. This makes our question clearer: Do all versions of pluralism have to accept that correct logic can be overtly relativized to subjective parameters like agent preferences? No. They do not. In fact, Shapiro's eclectic view is not relativistic in this sense, so he really does not disagree in any important way with Beall and Restall on this point.

In this section, we raised miscellaneous issues. What they have in common is that they revolve around various challenges to the robustness of logical pluralism. Some of these issues clearly deserve more attention, but we leave them for now.

## 3.3 The Meaning-Variance Worry

In the rest of this section, we scrutinize two pressing issues for logical pluralists. The first is the meaning-variance thesis. To reiterate, according to Quine (1986, p. 81), change of logic constitutes change of meaning. More carefully, logics that make different judgments about valid arguments involving the same symbol attribute different meanings to that symbol.

Quine vividly expresses the meaning-variance thesis in a famous passage where he envisions a debate in which one party advocates for paraconsistent logic against another party who accepts classical logic.

> My view of this dialogue is that neither party knows what he is talking about. They think they are talking about negation, '[¬]', 'not'; but surely the notation ceased to be recognizable as negation when they took to regarding some conjunctions of the form '[$p \wedge \neg p$]' as true, and stopped regarding such sentences as implying all others. Here, evidently, is the deviant logician's predicament: when he tries to deny the doctrine he only changes the subject.

Quine suggests here that theorists who attest different attitudes toward the principle of explosion must have different notions of negation in mind. Hjortland (2013) takes the point to be that these theorists are talking past one another. They do not have conflicting beliefs that can be unequivocally communicated in a shared language (compare Stei's worry in the previous section). If meaning-variance is true, then any debate between advocates of different logics becomes a "merely verbal" disagreement.

For Quine, there may be particularly good reasons to hold this view about the link between logic and meaning. He is a holist about meaning, so even the tiniest shift in one's attitude toward the assertibility of a sentence or the propriety of an inference has a knock-on effect on the meanings of every expression in one's language. If we want to reject or qualify the meaning-variance thesis, we have to reject semantic holism.

In the preceding passage, Quine suggests that this change of meaning phenomenon somehow diminishes support for non-classical logics and bolsters support for classical logic. That particular lesson is wrong. If meaning-variance creates situations of "merely verbal" disagreement, this does not just insulate classical logic from rational critique, it equally insulates any rival non-classical logic (see Priest (2006a) on this point). There is no specific view on correct logic that comes out ahead just in virtue of the meaning-variance thesis.

Meaning-variance has long been perceived as a latent threat to versions of pluralism that endorse different logics in the same language, but there are several issues to address here. Is the meaning-variance thesis really true? Do logical pluralists have to worry about this more than monists? If so, can pluralists answer the challenge?

Putnam (1969) and Haack (1996) deny the meaning-variance thesis, but they offer rather inconclusive arguments to this effect. It is a vexed issue in part because *meaning* is such a vexed issue. For this discussion to get off the ground, we have to understand logics in such a way that it is at least conceivable that there is a gap between their formal mechanisms and the meanings that are studied, modeled, or imparted by those mechanisms. How could this occur? We pointed out that idealization pluralists think of semantic models as intentionally imperfect representations of natural language meaning. That makes room for different logics to represent the same meaning, but of course it would be nice to know more about why this methodology is appropriate.

Field (2009) offers another observation from his expressivist approach. If logics are sets of epistemic norms, how do we track meanings between them? Field uses a *translation* strategy to map formulas from one logic onto another by looking for formulas that have the most similar overall role in logical laws. On this basis, a sentence of the form $\neg p$ in classical logic is most similar to $\neg p$ in relevant logic. A sentence of the form $\neg p$ in relevant logic is most similar to $p \to \bot$ in intuitionistic logic. But this is nontransitive: a sentence of the form $\neg p$ in classical logic is most similar to $\neg p$ in intuitionistic logic, rather than $p \to \bot$. He claims that "there is no notion of intertheoretic sameness of meaning" because if there were, it would be preserved under our best translations.

These views problematize the relationship between a logic and the meaning of its expressions. It is not crystal clear whether the meaning-variance thesis is true. However, meaning-variance has many defenders. Warren (2018) recently revitalized a version of the Quinean argument. We should not just brush the issue aside.

That brings us to another consideration. Assuming that meaning-variance is true, is it more of a problem for logical pluralists than for logical monists? Certainly not. It affects the philosophy of logic in general. Any logical monist who believes that her favorite logic is rationally defensible should worry about this issue. How can the monist criticize rival views about the nature of correct logic if she cannot avoid talking past her rivals? That is precisely what meaning-variance alleges, so it poses a problem for everyone.

However, the reason that pluralists have devoted so much energy to this topic is that many of them are strongly opposed to the meaning-variance thesis. We mentioned this in Section 2: The so-called *meaning-invariant* logical pluralists hold that a piece of logical vocabulary can have one meaning that manifests in different ways in different logics. This offensive maneuver aims to refute meaning-variance outright, but it is important to emphasize that not all pluralists share this aspiration.

Some pluralists consider meaning-variance to be unavoidable and unproblematic. For example, Kouri Kissel (2018) argues that mathematicians working on different versions of arithmetic sometimes use logical expressions with different meanings. She posits that the common ground (CG) of a conversation may include the Correlation as Identity (CI) assumption: If two words sound alike, are spelled the same way, and are generally used in the same sentences in the same way then they mean the same thing. If the CI is in the CG of a conversation, then the expressions of two theories with different logics can be treated as meaning the same thing (think: different theories of "number"). If the CI is dropped from the CG, then our words have different meanings. On this view, a logical term like negation is not individuated by a fixed meaning. So, what is a negation? That is a great question. Perhaps the best answer would run along functionalist lines: We recognize some kind of family resemblance by which two expressions with different meaning serve enough of the same functions that we classify them as versions of negation.

However, meaning-invariant pluralists aim to refute meaning-variance outright. To do so, they draw on considerations from independently plausible philosophical theories on the nature of meaning. One strategy argues that semantic models are *truth-conditional* theories of meaning. The problem is that, on the surface, this interpretation of model theory just feeds into the appearance of meaning-variance.

For example, the following clause looks like it is a good way to characterize the truth-conditions attributed to negation in the model theory for classical logic that we discussed in Section 1.4 (the $x$ ranges over classical models or cases):

$\neg p$ is true in $x$ if, and only if, $p$ is not true in $x$.

And the following clause is a good way to characterize the truth-conditions attributed to negation by intuitionistic logic (where $x, y$ range over constructions or epistemic stages):

$\neg p$ is true in $x$ if, and only if, $p$ is not true in any $y$ extending $x$.

These two clauses look quite different.

Restall (2002) argues, however, that there are other ways of understanding these models. There are several ways in which the evaluation policies of formal logics can be related to the explanatory notion of truth-conditions. A *minimalist* truth-condition is a Davidsonian "bare biconditional" that lacks any variable ranging over models or cases:

$\neg p$ is true if, and only if, $p$ is not true.

Restall claims that different formal evaluation clauses might be seen as *precisifications* of this minimal truth-condition. The concept of negation, characterized by the bare biconditional, might exhibit indeterminacy much like the GTT concept of validity. This may clarify the core meaning that is expressed by both logics in different ways.

On a similar note, Hjortland (2013) explores a *maximalist* approach to articulating truth-conditions (the terminology of calling these minimal versus maximal strategies comes originally from Restall, it is slightly different from terminology used by Hjortland). This strategy looks for a much more flexible, explicitly parameterized principle that has the classical and intuitionistic evaluation policies as special cases. Hjortland proposes:

$\neg p$ is true in $x$ if, and only if, $p$ is not true in any $y$ that is $R$-related to $x$.

This clause involves a variable $R$ which is not a variable over cases, but over different structural relations between cases. Then, intuitionistic logic instantiates this truth-condition over constructive stages with $R$ the relation of inclusion $\prec$, while classical logic instantiates the very same truth-condition over classical *models cum possible worlds* where $R$ is simply fulfilled by the identity relation from each model to itself.

Hjortland mentions this option only to reject it. He thinks these approaches are too sensitive to our choice of logics. This is not a general strategy for analyzing truth-conditions that will give us informative, general criteria for synonymy (see also Hjortland (2014)). But there are at least some tentative ideas in the spirit of truth-conditional semantics to account for invariant meaning across different logics.

The more promising attempt to refute meaning-variance comes from proof-theoretic pluralism. We discussed this in Section 2.5, but there is a lot more to say. On this approach, proof theory is an *inferentialist* or *conceptual role* theory of meaning. In other words, the meaning of $*$ consists in the network of conceptual relations between $*$-involving sentences and all other sentences that are articulated by the $*$ proof rules.

The technical details of this idea, carried out in the framework of sequent calculus, are clear enough, but we previously raised some questions about the philosophical foundations of this approach. Ferrari and Orlandelli (2021) offer some answers to those questions. First, they adopt exactly the same sequent calculus rules as Gentzen and Restall. Second, they say that we should understand the concept of proof encoded by these rules to be *primitive* and not one that can be justified in terms of its relation to external phenomena like truth, facts, models, belief, knowledge, and so on. This is not very helpful to the outsider who is hoping for some insight into *why* we should accept this rule set, or the corresponding concept of proof, but at least it takes a clear stance on the nature of the concept.

Finally, Ferrari and Orlandelli propose that *harmony* is a criterion of logical correctness within this proof theory. This is a technical term that we won't entirely try to define, but it is easily motivated by the famous example of Prior (1960). Imagine you adopt an arbitrary pair of rules for the expression "tonk":

$$\frac{\Gamma \Rightarrow p}{\Gamma \Rightarrow p\text{-tonk-}q} \qquad \frac{\Gamma \Rightarrow p\text{-tonk-}q}{\Gamma \Rightarrow q}$$

These are terrible rules. From any commitment $p$ that you really believe is true, you can infer any random $q$ using the tonk rules. This would allow us "get out" much more information than was "put in" by the original set of premises. Being able to get out more than you put in is the characteristic feature of *unharmonious* rules. Even within the sequent calculus rules that we described previously, there are ways to drop one rule or a few. Some of these combinations would be unharmonious. The correct logics are the ones that are defined by harmonious subsets of the standard sequent rules.

In addition to the logics endorsed by Restall, this version of proof-theoretic pluralism also endorses some relevant logics and noncontractive, substructural logics. By making the criteria of correctness more explicit, this view also clarifies the biggest question for the proof-theoretic pluralist. This view refutes meaning-variance by adopting a *molecular* perspective on meaning. Some proof rules are meaning-determining, others are not. In particular, for Ferrari and Orlandelli, structural rules of sequent calculus like the rule of weakening are not meaning-determining. Only the operational rules that directly govern specific logical terms are considered to be meaning-determining rules. This not only permits the variations in derivational policies that were mentioned in connection with Gentzen and Restall (Section 2.5), as well as other such variations, but also explains precisely why those variations do not affect the meaning of the logical terms: *they don't affect harmony*.

This view draws from a plausible theory of meaning to draw a distinction between aspects of proof theory that are essential to meaning and those that are not. Different logics, with different extensional definitions of proof, can be said to share the same meanings of the operators because they share meaning-determining rules. It is an ambitious attempt to refute meaning-variance and defend meaning-invariance.

However, there is a lingering issue that muddies the water. We saw how Gentzen's proof theory is the basis for a view that there are many logics with shared meanings. These are different realizations of a single concept of proof. Call this Plurality #1. We have mentioned that other, similar results exist in the literature. For example, both Hjortland (2013) and Shapiro (2017) develop proof theories in which classical logic, K3, LP, and FDE can be defined by varying incidental features of the system. Such proof theory is the basis for another view on which there are many logics with shared meanings. These logics also plausibly realize a single concept of proof. Call this Plurality #2.

The problem is this: Plurality #1 assigns a meaning to negation, which is invariant across that group of logics, and Plurality #2 assigns a meaning to negation, which is invariant across that group of logics, but the first meaning (rule set) is not the same as the second meaning (rule set). Which system captures the *real* negation and the *real* concept of proofs? A better philosophical account of the extrasystemic phenomena might single out a privileged formulation of proof theory and answer this challenge.

Ferrari and Orlandelli are aware of this issue, but they do not want to handle it by giving a substantive definition of the extrasystemic phenomena. Instead, they claim that we have to rely on pragmatic or holistic criteria to choose between pluralities of logics that attribute different meanings to logical operators. Perhaps this is something like Field's view on which choice of (a plurality of) logics is shaped by one's epistemic goals.

# Logical Pluralism

The final package view shares something of the spirit of Carnapian pluralism, but it updates that view because it draws firmer limits around what can count as a correct logic. The plurality we accept is somewhat conventional, but since logics must be harmonious, not just any plurality of logics will be a viable option. The remaining question is whether a view that bottoms out in pragmatism solves the meaning-variance worry in the way we *wanted* it to be solved. That is a topic for future research.

## 3.4 The Normative Collapse Problem

We said from the start that it is good for arguments to be valid, and proofs are instances of good reasoning. Logic seems to have epistemic value, but it is not entirely straightforward to specify the role it plays in rational belief formation.

Some people are skeptical of such a connection. Harman (1984, 1986) considers and rejects the following type of principle that purports to describe how validity bears on what we ought to believe ("INF" for "infer"):

**INF:** For any valid argument from premises $p_1, \ldots, p_n$ to conclusion $q$, if any agent $S$ believes all of $p_1, \ldots, p_n$, then $S$ ought to believe $q$.

Why does Harman reject INF? Consider the issue of *excessive demands*: if you believe the Peano Axioms for arithmetic, then according to INF you ought to infer every single theorem of PA, but this includes an infinite number of theorems many of which are not even useful to know. If rational belief is bounded by our goals and limited resources, then INF simply looks wrong. It suggests norms that do not apply to creatures like us.

Steinberger (2019a) adapts a framework from MacFarlane (2004) to confront this strand of skepticism. In the literature, INF is called a bridge principle: a type of principle that proposes a systematic relationship between valid arguments and norms of belief. In this discussion, it is typically assumed that invalidity does not have the same significance as validity. The reason is that inductive, probabilistic, scientific arguments can be good arguments even though by nature, they are often invalid simply because they are not *trying* to be completely airtight in the same way as deductively valid arguments. Put another way: invalid reasoning is not *bad* reasoning per se. The fact that an argument is invalid just does not seem to have interesting, normative significance in itself.

Steinberger discusses many ways of modifying the pattern of INF to yield all sorts of different bridge principles. These modifications can be more or less plausible depending on details. Some bridge principles avoid aspects of Harmanian sketpicism and, to that extent, they offer more promising ways in which to explicate the normative role of logic.

One way in which we can modify INF is to soften the deontic operator. Instead of thinking of validity as a source of outright epistemic obligations, we might think of it as a source of something less forceful such as *defeasible reasons* for belief:

**DEF:** If the argument from premises $p_1, \ldots, p_n$ to conclusion $q$ is valid,
if any agent $S$ believes all of $p_1, \ldots, p_n$, then $S$ has reason to believe $q$.

Notice that DEF does not impose excessive demands. Suppose that $S$'s beliefs logically imply $q$, but she does not currently believe $q$. Then $S$ has *some reason* to infer $q$ according to DEF. Let's call this a logic-based reason. However, this is one consideration in a larger process of weighing evidence. It can be overridden by other reasons. If $S$ ultimately has overriding reasons not to believe $q$, then her logic-based reasons do not in themselves compel her to do anything. So, DEF is a less demanding bridge principle.

Another way in which we can modify INF is to change how we express the scope of the normative constraint. Instead of expecting guidance about what to infer in the next moment, we might instead look for logical *evaluation* of our belief state at a single moment in time. This kind of bridge principle will describe the minimal conditions for rational belief. A belief state with an internal logical clash is irrational:

**EVAL:** For any valid argument from premises $p_1, \ldots, p_n$ to conclusion $q$,
no agent $S$ ought to believe all of $p_1, \ldots, p_n$ and disbelieve $q$.

EVAL does not impose excessive demands either. Suppose that $S$'s beliefs imply $q$, but $S$ has simply never considered $q$ and has no attitude toward it, either positive or negative. A lack of opinion does not clash with anything, so this belief state is minimally rational according to EVAL, which means that $S$ is under no demand to change anything. So, once again, we have a less demanding bridge principle than INF.

Suffice to say, there are various ways to think about the epistemic value of logic that improve on INF. We leave aside the details and turn to a schematic representation of *whatever* bridge principle truly captures the normative role of validity:

**BRIDGE:** If the argument from premises $p_1, \ldots, p_n$ to conclusion $q$ is valid,
then Norm$(p_1, \ldots, p_n, q)$ applies to all agents.

If we accept a particular logic, which demarcates a set of valid arguments, then BRIDGE implies that all and only those arguments serve the target epistemic Norm. Call this the *normative profile* of our accepted logic.

A logical pluralist accepts more than one logic $L_1, \ldots, L_k$. The foregoing discussion of bridge principles suggests that each of these logics has its own

## Logical Pluralism

normative profile. So, the pluralist is committed to a plurality of logic-based norms $N_1, \ldots, N_k$. It has been argued that this situation leads to a *normative collapse problem* for logical pluralism (Priest, 2001; Read, 2006; Keefe, 2014; Caret, 2017; Kellen, 2020; Stei, 2020b).

The problem turns on three claims. First, the claim that it is possible to satisfy $N_1, \ldots, N_k$ all at once by conforming to a single normative profile $N$. Second, the claim that $N$ coincides with the normative profile of a particular logic $L$. Finally, the critic claims that this commits the pluralist to logical monism, which of course undermines her view (see Caret (2017); Stei (2020b)). If all three claims are true, then logical pluralism is unsustainable. We will work our way up to a nuanced analysis of this dramatic attack on logical pluralism, but first we should point out how the first two steps work.

Williamson (1988, p. 122) sets up the collapse problem by imagining distinct correct logics and then asking, "[if] your beliefs...have a certain consequence in the sense of one but not in the sense of the other; should you accept that consequence or not?." This question implicitly assumes something like INF as the right bridge principle. This formulation does not necessarily pose an overwhelming problem.

Suppose that logics $L1$ and $L2$ are correct and that $p \vdash_{L1} q$ but $p \nvdash_{L2} q$. We present this in the form of a single-premise argument for simplicity. Nothing important rests on that simplification. The important point is that these two logics make different judgments about the very same argument. Call this a *divergence* case. (One thing we are assuming is that the logical pluralist does not have to deal with cases where $p \vdash_{L1} q$ and $p \vdash_{L2} \neg q$, which is true for most influential pluralist views.) Williamson asks what to do in a divergence case, but since he is assuming INF, the answer is quite straightforward: Since the argument is valid one way, INF tells us that we should draw the inference. That would be the end of the story and there would be no deep problem to contend with.

However, we might start to wonder if this question poses a more difficult challenge when we assume a more philosophically plausible reading of BRIDGE. In schematic form, the question becomes "Should you conform to Norm$(p, q)$ or not?" But it still looks as if the answer is just as straightforward as previously: Since the argument is valid one way, BRIDGE tells us that we should conform to this norm.

This brings us to the real problem. In the previous discussion, we can see how the logical pluralist is faced with a commitment to various logic-based normative demands, but she often has a dominant strategy for satisfying these demands. For the pluralist, in any divergence case, there is one logic that says the target argument is valid and which places a normative constraint on belief, while the other logic does not place any constraint. This makes room for a master argument that supports the first step toward collapse, namely, the claim that we can reduce all of $N_1, \ldots, N_k$ to a single normative profile $N$.

Keefe (2014, p. 1385) proposes a method for defining a privileged normative profile on any pluralist view. Given a plurality of correct logics: Norm$(p,q)$ applies to all agents if, and only if, the argument $p \vdash q$ is valid according to at least one logic in the plurality. In other words, this principle collects all of the norms that flow from this logic or that logic or the other logic. Call this a *disjunctive normative profile*, $N$. We can see that $N$ is just an amalgam of norms. It is meant to partly flow from different sources and it does not necessarily have unified grounds. However, the important initial observation is this: If any correct logic imposes a norm pertaining to some specific form of reasoning, then $N$ imposes exactly the same norm. So, by conforming to this disjunctive normative profile, we would successfully conform to each of the individual normative profiles in the plurality $N_1, \ldots, N_k$. This finishes the first step toward collapse.

The second step links $N$ to a particular logic. It is relatively easy to turn this trick at the extensional level. We are thinking about logics $L_1, \ldots, L_k$ that give extensionally distinct accounts of validity over the same formal language. Such logics are distinguished by different judgments they make about the validity of specific argument forms. If we are only interested in an extensional definition of validity, we can combine every instance of $L_1$ validity and $L_2$ validity and…and $L_k$ validity to define a logic $L$ *at least as strong* as each logic in the plurality. The normative profile of $L$ via BRIDGE coincides exactly with the disjunctive normative profile $N$ defined by Keefe's recipe given earlier.

However, it is important at this point to pause and highlight a question that might short-circuit the collapse problem. Does the pluralist have to accept $L$? The answer to this question is often "yes," but this is not inevitable.

Gooßens and Tedder (2023) point out a hypothetical version of logical pluralism on which the pluralist should not accept this "strongest" logic $L$ for principled reasons. Consider a pluralist who generally believes that only relevant logics are correct. She believes that a relevance requirement is essential to logic. However, she accepts a plurality of different logics that meet this requirement (we mentioned in Section 1.4 that there are various relevant logics that slightly differ in how they handle conditional formulas). Gooßens and Tedder observe that this form of pluralism can accept different relevant logics whose extensional combination produces an *irrelevant* logic $L$. For this pluralist, the collapse problem would never really go through. The problem requires a commitment to $N$ on the normative side, and a commitment to $L$ within the category of correct logics, but the pluralist we just mentioned rejects $L$ from this category. This interesting thought experiment indicates what a stable form of logical pluralism could look like.

Nonetheless, the view we have just described is highly hypothetical and quite different from the versions of logical pluralism that are most prominent in the philosophical literature. In particular, the most vocal logical pluralists cannot avoid the collapse problem in the way we have just discussed because they explicitly accept a strongest logic. Beall and Restall (2006), Restall (2014), and Shapiro (2014b) each endorse a range of logics that includes at most classical logic and some of its sublogics, like the intuitionistic and relevant logics we surveyed in Section 1. The disjunctive normative profile of such a pluralist view coincides exactly with the profile of classical logic. That finishes the second step toward collapse.

Is it inherently problematic for the pluralist to admit that one logic is generally informative about all logical norms? Suppose the dominant logic is classical logic for the sake of concreteness. We may find this situation more or less surprising depending on the kind of bridge principle we find most plausible.

If we accept DEF we may think that different logics are sources of different kinds of reasons for belief. In general, we can acquire reasons to believe one statement from many sources. On this understanding, the dominance of classical logic would just amount to the view that classical logic is often a redundant source of logic-based reasons that also issue from other logics, but that does not sound like a huge problem in itself. However, what if we accept EVAL instead? Then we think of logic as normatively issuing unqualified bans against belief states that are internally defective because they are not even minimally rational. On this understanding, the dominance of classical logic is more worrying because it looks like that logic plays a privileged role in defining the structure of logically irrational, banned beliefs. Other logics seem to be normatively impotent on such a view. The point is that the reading of BRIDGE can make a difference to the seriousness of the normative collapse problem.

One way to defuse all such worries is to draw a much firmer line between logic and norms. Russell (2020) and Blake-Turner and Russell (2021) develop a *nonnormative* view of logic and relate this to logical pluralism. They consider a logical theory to consist in a description of logical laws, much like science is a description of natural laws. A descriptive theory makes no mention of norms, and by Hume's law, it has no intrinsic normative implications. Bridge principles seem intuitive to us because we combined the descriptive content of logic with other things we believe, such as a normative theory about the aim of belief. Such a pluralist may admit a strongest logic $L$, which corresponds with disjunctive normative profile $N$, but she might say that this is an *extralogical* commitment.

It does not impact her pluralist view of logics because the normative question is an issue in epistemology, not an issue in the discipline of logic itself.

Stei (2023) argues that a puzzle about normativity reemerges for this view so long as truth is essential to the characterization of logic. Even if norms are not part of the content of logic, once we turn to using logic we will still converge on a single logical system that generally serves this purpose. However, the talk of using logic gives away the game. The most important idea of nonnormativist pluralism is to divest normativity from any role in settling which logics are correct. Stei concedes this is possible and admits that he is not trying to attack the stability of such a pluralist view. Then, whatever issue he is raising, it does not clearly pose a threat to this kind of nonnormativist pluralism.

However, we now want to consider the strongest version of collapse. This follows from the claim that epistemic normativity is *criterial* of correct logic. To dramatize the point, suppose we are uncertain about which logic is correct and we look for guidance in the form of some philosophical criteria. How is the appeal to normativity supposed to help? We might spell out the purpose of this criterion as follows. According to our pretheoretic understanding, one distinctive feature of logic is that it fulfills the antecedent conditions in BRIDGE and thereby issues logic-based norms of belief. Logic is *the kind of thing* that is suited to issue such norms. This implies that a logic that provides more information about logical norms scores best on the normativity criterion. If a pluralist accepts this criterion and she accepts a logic $L$ that provides the most general information about logical norms (by steps one and two earlier), then other things being equal, this pluralist is committed to view $L$ as *uniquely correct* – The One True Logic.

As we have seen, it is possible for a logical pluralist to avoid the second step to collapse (reject $L$) and it is possible to avoid the third step (nonnormative pluralism). Total collapse only threatens pluralist views that support all three of the previous steps. The most feasible example in the literature is the view of Beall and Restall (2006).

Other pluralists' views come dangerously close to this problem, but they may try to avoid the full impact by relativizing correct logic to contexts or discourse domains. This effectively bifurcates the view: In any context or domain we have monism, but from a philosophical outsider perspective we acknowledge many contexts or domains with their own correct logics. If the normative role of logics can be isolated into separate contexts or domains, then divergence cases do not exist and the collapse problem never gets started. Kouri Kissel and Shapiro (2020) suggest that this might safeguard their eclectic version of logical pluralism against collapse. Bueno and Shalkowksi accept some domain-relativity as part of their modalist pluralism. In Section 2.7 we mentioned a contextualist modification of case-based pluralism (Caret, 2017). On this view, the content of BRIDGE is relativized to each context of inquiry. The epistemic goals of a context determine a uniquely correct logic for that context, which may differ from the correct logic of another context.

The biggest problem with those solutions is that they give up one of the traditional aspirations of the study of logic. According to tradition, logic should be *universal* and *topic-neutral*. If logic is relativized to contexts or discourse domains, are we really talking about logic anymore? This is a trade-off that many pluralists struggle with.

Tajer (2022) proposes a different response to collapse: that bridge principles should be pluralized. If there are multiple bridge principles, there are also competing norms about how logic(s) pertain to defeasible reasons for belief and what kind of belief states are rationally permissible. This allows norms issued by a logically weaker system to sometimes have epistemic priority over norms from a logically stronger system. It no longer makes sense to even speak of a disjunctive normative profile that captures all of these norms.

Steinberger (2019b) calls the preceding problem *upward* collapse. Steinberger argues that a different problem of *downward* collapse threatens domain-relative versions of pluralism. The thought runs as follows. For domain-relative pluralists, BRIDGE can be relativized to each domain, but in mixed domains, modesty requires that the governing norms come from the weakest logic of any individual domain. This can be generalized as follows: agents should conform to Norm($p,q$) if, and only if, the argument $p \vdash q$ is valid in every correct logic. This general normative profile works in every domain, but it aligns with the weakest logic in the plurality, thus we have another route to logical monism.

There is no simple way to summarize the normative collapse problem. It is complicated by many things. Logical pluralists disagree among themselves about the nature of logic, including how normativity gets into the picture. They disagree about which specific norms flow from logic and why. Perhaps the best way to understand the collapse problem is analogous to the role of radical skepticism in contemporary epistemology: Total collapse is a well-known problem that any stable version of logical pluralism must avoid. There are ongoing debates about how best to achieve that.

## Final Thoughts

Logic is the study of validity and proofs. It indirectly demarcates trivial theories. We want our arguments to be valid and our theories non-trivial. This makes logic important.

Modern logics offer formal accounts of validity and proofs, built on formal languages with explicit categories of logical vocabulary. Logical pluralism says that more than one logic is correct, which can sound quite unusual at first. In fact, there is a plurality of pluralisms. Hopefully, you come away from this Element with the impression that at least some versions of logical pluralism are interesting, coherent, and defensible philosophical views. The question remains whether any them are sufficiently robust or true.

In closing out this Element, we draw attention to a few topics that deserve further thought and point the way toward future research. In no particular order:

- **Pluralism and Objectivity**: Pluralists want to resist any method of consolidating logics under a single banner, sliding into logical monism. This resistance is often expressed by a "no fact of the matter" claim: there is no fact of the matter about how to demarcate logical vocabulary, no fact of the matter about how to define "case" in general, no fact of the matter about what all mathematical structures have in common. This is not always emphasized, but the picture of a disparate, fragmented plurality requires some such claim to be true. It is worth thinking about what these "no fact" claims mean and whether they have problematic metaphysical implications.
- **Pluralism and Natural Language**: In light of modern logical methods, it can be tempting to drive a wedge between logic and natural language. Contrary to the traditional study of informal discourse, some modern logicians only have an interest in mathematical reasoning. Just as often, however, we see trends in logic that mostly draw inspiration from natural language evidence (modal, relevant, and counterfactual logics). The exact relationship between these topics is important to most pluralists, yet these views do not always have a lot to say about natural language: Is it inherently different from formal language, is natural language only imperfectly "formalizable," and why think so?
- **Pluralism and Metalogic**: We have danced around the issue of formality, often tied up with the idea of logic as a "general, all purpose" theory. This might lead us to think that a correct logic captures universal laws that apply even in our mathematical framework for defining formal logics. At the metalogical level, where we "do logic," it is common to rely on a well-established part of classical mathematics like iterative set theory (ZF). Griffiths and Paseau (2022) argue if pluralism is true, we should be able to do metalogical reasoning in any correct logic, but this is practically impossible on most pluralist views. They conclude that logical monism is true. It is a kind of transcendental argument: that there must be a uniquely correct logic, some extension of classical first-order logic, which is suitable as its own metalogic. These are difficult technical issues to think through.

At any rate, these pointers should make one thing clear: there is a lot more to think about and the debate over logical pluralism is far from finished.

# References

Anderson, Alan Ross and Belnap, Nuel D., Jr. 1962. "The Pure Calculus of Entailment." *Journal of Symbolic Logic* 27:19–52.

——— 1975. *Entailment: The Logic of Relevance and Necessity*, volume I. Princeton University Press.

Antonsen, Paal Fjeldvig. 2025. "Logical Contextualism." *Inquiry* 68:854–873. www.tandfonline.com/doi/full/10.1080/0020174X.2022.2075917.

Barwise, Jon and Perry, John. 1983. *Situations and Attitudes*. MIT Press.

Beall, Jc. 2009. *Spandrels of Truth*. Oxford University Press.

Beall, Jc and Restall, Greg. 2000. "Logical Pluralism." *Australasian Journal of Philosophy* 78:475–493.

——— 2006. *Logical Pluralism*. Oxford University Press.

Belnap, Nuel. 1992. "How a Computer Should Think." In Alan Ross Anderson, Nuel Belnap Jr., and J. Michael Dunn (eds.), *Entailment: The Logic of Relevance and Necessity*, volume II, 506–541. Princeton University Press.

Blake-Turner, Christopher and Russell, Gillian. 2021. "Logical Pluralism without the Normativity." *Synthese* 198:4859–4877.

Bonnay, Denis. 2008. "Logicality and Invariance." *The Bulletin of Symbolic Logic* 14:29–68.

Brandom, Robert B. 1994. *Making It Explicit: Reasoning, Representing, and Discursive Commitment*. Harvard University Press.

Bremer, Manuel. 2014. "Restall and Beall on Logical Pluralism: A Critique." *Erkenntnis* 79:293–299.

Brouwer, LEJ. 1908. "De Onbetrouwbaarheid der Logische Principes." *Tijdschrift voor Wijsbegeerte* 2:152–158. Translated as Brouwer (1975).

——— 1975. "The Unreliability of the Logical Principles." In Arend Heyting (ed.), *L. E. J. Brouwer Collected Works, vol. I: Philosophy and Foundations of Mathematics*, 107–111. North-Holland.

Bueno, Otávio and Shalkowski, Scott A. 2009. "Modalism and Logical Pluralism." *Mind* 118:295–321.

Caret, Colin R. 2017. "The Collapse of Logical Pluralism Has Been Greatly Exaggerated." *Erkenntnis* 82:739–760.

——— 2021. "Why Logical Pluralism?" *Synthese* 198:4947–4968.

Caret, Colin R. and Hjortland, Ole T. (eds.). 2015. *Foundations of Logical Consequence*. Oxford University Press.

Carnap, Rudolf. 1937. *Logical Syntax of Language*. Kegan Paul, Trench, Trubner & Co. Amethe Smeaton (trans.).

1950. "Empiricism, Semantics, and Ontology." *Revue Internationale de Philosophie* 4:20–40.

Cohen, Stewart. 1988. "How to Be a Fallibilist." *Philosophical Perspectives* 2:91–123.

Cook, Roy T. 2002. "Vagueness and Mathematical Precision." *Mind* 111:225–247.

2010. "Let a Thousand Flowers Bloom: A Tour of Logical Pluralism." *Philosophy Compass* 5:492–504.

Cotnoir, Aaron J. 2018. "Logical Nihilism." In Jeremy Wyatt, Nikolaj Jang Lee Linding Pedersen, and Nathan Kellen (eds.), *Pluralisms in Truth and Logic*, 301–330. Palgrave Macmillan.

DeRose, Keith. 1992. "Contextualism and Knowledge Attributions." *Philosophy and Phenomenological Research* 52:913–929.

Dicher, Bogdan. 2020. "Variations on Intra-theoretical Logical Pluralism: Internal Versus External Consequence." *Philosophical Studies* 177:667–686.

Dummett, Michael. 1959. "Truth." *Proceedings of the Aristotelian Society* 59:141–162.

1978. *Truth and Other Enigmas*. Harvard University Press.

1991. *The Logical Basis of Metaphysics*. Harvard University Press.

Eklund, Matti. 2020. "Making Sense of Logical Pluralism." *Inquiry* 62:433–454.

Ferrari, Filippo and Moruzzi, Sebastiano. 2020. "Logical Pluralism, Indeterminacy and the Normativity of Logic." *Inquiry* 63:282–301.

Ferrari, Filippo and Orlandelli, Eugenio. 2021. "Proof-theoretic Pluralism." *Synthese* 198:4879–4903.

Field, Hartry. 2009. "Pluralism in Logic." *The Review of Symbolic Logic* 2: 342–359.

2015. "What Is Logical Validity?" In Caret and Hjortland (2015), 33–70.

Frege, Gottlob. 1879. *Begriffsschrift: eine der arithmetischen nachgebildete Formelsprache des reinen Denkens*. Verlag von Louis Nebert. Translated as Frege (1967).

1967. "Begriffsschrift, a Formula Language, Modeled upon That of Arithmetic, for Pure Thought." In Jean van Heijenoort (ed.), *From Frege to Gödel: A Source Book in Mathematical Logic, 1879–1931*, 1–82. Harvard University Press. S. Bauer-Mengelberg (trans.).

Gentzen, Gerhard. 1969. "Investigations into Logical Deduction." In ME Szabo (ed.), *The Collected Papers of Gerhard Gentzen*, 68–131. North-Holland. Original version 1935.

Girard, Jean-Yves. 1987. "Linear Logic." *Theoretical Computer Science* 50: 1–102.

Glanzberg, Michael. 2015. "Logical Consequence and Natural Language." In Caret and Hjortland (2015), 71–120.

2021. "Models, Model Theory, and Modeling." In Gil Sagi and Jack Woods (eds.), *The Semantic Conception of Logic: Essays on Consequence, Invariance, and Meaning*, 209–226. Cambridge University Press.

Goddu, G. C. 2002. "What Exactly Is Logical Pluralism?" *Australasian Journal of Philosophy* 80:218–230.

Gooßens, Dustin and Tedder, Andrew. 2023. "No Cause for Collapse." *Asian Journal of Philosophy* 2(37). DOI: https://doi.org/10.1007/s44204-023-00083-1.

Griffiths, Owen. 2013. "Problems for Logical Pluralism." *History and Philosophy of Logic* 34:170–182.

Griffiths, Owen and Paseau, A. C. 2022. *One True Logic: A Monist Manifesto*. Oxford University Press.

Haack, Susan. 1978. *Philosophy of Logics*. Cambridge University Press.

1996. *Deviant Logic, Fuzzy Logic: Beyond the Formalism*. The University of Chicago Press.

Harman, Gilbert. 1984. "Logic and Reasoning." *Synthese* 60:107–127.

1986. *Change in View: Principles of Reasoning*. MIT Press.

Heim, Irene and Kratzer, Angelika. 1998. *Semantics in Generative Grammar*. Blackwell.

Hellman, Geoffrey. 2006. "Mathematical Pluralism: The Case of Smooth Infinitesimal Analysis." *Journal of Philosophical Logic* 35:621–651.

Heyting, Arend. 1930. "Die formalen Regeln der intuitionistischen Logik." *Sitzungsberichte der Preussischen Akademie der Wissenschaften* 42–71, 158–169. Deütsche Akademie der Wissenschaften zu Berlin, Mathematisch-Naturwissenschaftliche Klasse. Translated as Heyting (1998).

1998. "The Formal Rules of Intuitionistic Logic." In Paolo Mancuso (ed.), *From Brouwer to Hilbert: The Debate on the Foundations of Mathematics in the 1920s*, 311–327. Oxford University Press.

Hjortland, Ole Thomassen. 2013. "Logical Pluralism, Meaning-Variance, and Verbal Disputes." *Australasian Journal of Philosophy* 91:355–373.

2014. "Verbal Disputes in Logic: Against Minimalism for Logical Connectives." *Logique et Analyse* 57:463–486.

Humberstone, Lloyd. 2011. *The Connectives*. MIT Press.

Kaplan, David. 1979. "On the Logic of Demonstratives." *Journal of Philosophical Logic* 8:81–98.

1989. "Demonstratives." In Joseph Almog, John Perry, and Howard Wettstein (eds.), *Themes from Kaplan*. Oxford University Press.

Keefe, Rosanna. 2014. "What Logical Pluralism Cannot Be." *Synthese* 191:1375–1390.

Kellen, Nathan. 2020. "The Normative Problem for Logical Pluralism." *Inquiry* 63:258–281.

Korzybski, Alfred. 1931. "A Non-Aristotelian System and Its Necessity for Rigour in Mathematics and Physics." Presented at the AMS meeting of 1931, later reprinted as an appendix of *Science and Sanity*, Lancaster, PA: Science Press Printing Company, 1933.

Kouri, Teresa. 2016. "Restall's Proof-Theoretic Pluralism and Relevance Logic." *Erkenntnis* 81:1243–1252.

Kouri Kissel, Teresa. 2018. "Logical Pluralism from a Pragmatic Perspective." *Australasian Journal of Philosophy* 96:578–591.

2021. "Metalinguistic Negotiation and Logical Pluralism." *Synthese* 198:4801–4812.

Kouri Kissel, Teresa and Shapiro, Stewart. 2020. "Logical Pluralism and Normativity." *Inquiry* 63:389–410.

Kratzer, Angelika. 2023. "Situations in Natural Language Semantics." In Edward N. Zalta (ed.), *The Stanford Encyclopedia of Philosophy*. CSLI Publications.

Kripke, Saul. 1982. *Wittgenstein on Rules and Private Language*. Harvard University Press.

Lewis, David. 1996. "Elusive Knowledge." *Australasian Journal of Philosophy* 74:549–567.

Łukasiewicz, Jan. 1936. "Logistyka a Filozofia." *Przegląd Filozoficzny* 39:115–131. Page numbers are from the English translation, reprinted as Łukasiewicz (1970).

1970. "Logistic and Philosophy." In Ludwik Borkowski (ed.), *Jan Łukasiewicz: Selected Works*, 218–235. North-Holland.

Lycan, William G. 1989. "Logical Constants and the Glory of Truth-Conditional Semantics." *Notre Dame Journal of Formal Logic* 30:390–400.

Lynch, Michael P. 2009. *Truth as One and Many*. Oxford University Press.

MacFarlane, John. 2004. "In What Sense (If Any) Is Logic Normative for Thought?" Unpublished draft. http://johnmacfarlane.net/work.html.

2014. *Assessment Sensitivity: Relative Truth and Its Applications*. Oxford University Press.

Mares, Edwin D. 2004. *Relevant Logic: A Philosophical Interpretation*. Cambridge University Press.

# References

Martin, Ben and Hjortland, Ole. 2021. "Logical Predictivism." *The Journal of Philosophical Logic* 50:285–318.

Pedersen, Nikolaj Jang Lee Linding. 2014. "Pluralism x 3: Truth, Logic, Metaphysics." *Erkenntnis* 79:259–277.

Priest, Graham. 2001. "Logic: One or Many?" In John Woods and Bryson Brown (eds.), *Logical Consequences: Rival Approaches*, 23–38. Hermes Scientific Publishers.

2006a. *Doubt Truth to be a Liar*. Oxford University Press.

2006b. *In Contradiction: A Study of the Transconsistent*. Oxford University Press, 2nd edition.

2008. *An Introduction to Non-Classical Logic: From If to Is*. Cambridge University Press.

2021. "A Note on Mathematical Pluralism and Logical Pluralism." *Synthese* 198:4937–4946.

Prior, A. N. 1960. "The Runabout Inference-Ticket." *Analysis* 21:38–39.

Putnam, Hilary. 1969. "Is Logic Empirical?" In Robert S. Cohen and Marx W. Wartofsky (eds.), *Boston Studies in the Philosophy of Science*, volume V, 216–241. Reidel.

Quine, W. V. 1986. *Philosophy of Logic*. Harvard University Press, 2nd edition.

Read, Stephen. 1988. *Relevant Logic: A Philosophical Examination of Inference*. Basil Blackwell Ltd.

2006. "Monism: The One True Logic." In David DeVidi and Tim Kenyon (eds.), *A Logical Approach to Philosophy: Essays in Honour of Graham Solomon*, 193–209. Springer.

Rescher, Nicholas and Manor, Ruth. 1970. "On Inference from Inconsistent Premisses." *Theory and Decision* 1:179–219.

Restall, Greg. 1996. "Information Flow and Relevant Logics." In Jerry Seligman and Dag Westerståhl (eds.), *Logic, Language and Computation*, CSLI Lecture Notes no. 58, 463–477. CSLI Publications.

2002. "Carnap's Tolerance, Meaning, and Logical Pluralism." *Journal of Philosophy* 99:426–443.

2005. "Multiple Conclusions." In Petr Hájek, Luis Valdés-Villanueva, and Dag Westerståhl (eds.), *Logic, Methodology and Philosophy of Science: Proceedings of the Twelfth International Congress*, 189–205. London: College Publications.

2014. "Pluralism and Proofs." *Erkenntnis* 79:279–291.

Ripley, David. 2012. "Conservatively Extending Classical Logic with Transparent Truth." *The Review of Symbolic Logic* 5:354–378.

Russell, Bertrand. 1903. *The Principles of Mathematics*. Cambridge University Press.

Russell, Gillian. 2008. "One True Logic?" *Journal of Philosophical Logic* 37:593–611.

2020. "Logic Isn't Normative." *Inquiry* 63:371–388.

2021. "Logical Pluralism." In Edward N. Zalta (ed.), *The Stanford Encyclopedia of Philosophy*. CSLI Publications.

Shalkowski, Scott A. 1994. "The Ontological Ground of the Alethic Modality." *The Philosophical Review* 103:669–688.

Shapiro, Lionel. 2017. "LP, K3, and FDE as substructural logics." In Pavel Arazim and Tomas Lávika (eds.), *The Logica Yearbook 2016*, 257–272. College Publications.

Shapiro, Stewart. 2011. "Varieties of Pluralism and Relativism for Logic." In Steven D. Hales (ed.), *A Companion to Relativism*, 526–552. Wiley-Blackwell.

2014a. "Structures and Logics: A Case for (a) Relativism." *Erkenntnis* 79:309–329.

2014b. *Varieties of Logic*. Oxford University Press.

Sher, Gila. 1991. *The Bounds of Logic: A Generalized Viewpoint*. MIT Press.

2022. *Logical Consequence*. Elements in Philosophy and Logic. Cambridge University Press.

Smith, Robin. 1989. *Aristotle's Prior Analytics*. Hackett.

Stei, Erik. 2020a. "Disagreement About Logic From a Pluralist Perspective." *Philosophical Studies* 177:3329–3350.

2020b. "Rivalry, Normativity, and the Collapse of Logical Pluralism." *Inquiry* 63:411–432.

2023. *Logical Pluralism and Logical Consequence*. Cambridge University Press.

Steinberger, Florian. 2019a. "Consequence and Normative Guidance." *Philosophy and Phenomenological Research* 98:306–328.

2019b. "Logical Pluralism and Logical Normativity." *Philosophers' Imprint* 19:1–19.

Tajer, Diego. 2022. "A Simple Solution to the Collapse Argument for Logical Pluralism." *Inquiry*.

Tarski, Alfred. 1933. "Pojęcie prawdy w językach nauk dedukcyjnych." Nakładem Towarzystwa Naukowego Warszawskiego.

1936. "Über den Begriff der logischen Folgerung." In *Actes du Congrès International de Philosophie Scientifique, Sorbonne, Paris, 1935*. Hermann. Translated as Tarski (2002).

1944. "The Semantic Conception of Truth: And the Foundations of Semantics." *Philosophy and Phenomenological Research* 4:341–376.

1986. "What Are Logical Notions?" *History and Philosophy of Logic* 7: 143–154. John Corcoran (editor).

2002. "On the Concept of Following Logically." *History and Philosophy of Logic* 23:155–196. Magda Stroińska and David Hitchcock (trans.).

Terrés Villalonga, Pilar. 2019. "From Natural to Formal Language: A Case for Logical Pluralism." *Topoi* 33:333–345.

Varzi, Achille C. 2002. "On Logical Relativity." *Philosophical Issues* 12:197–219.

Warren, Jarred. 2018. "Change of Logic, Change of Meaning." *Philosophy and Phenomenological Research* 96:421–442.

Williamson, Timothy. 1988. "Equivocation and Existence." *Proceedings of the Aristotelian Society* 88:109–127.

2014. "Logic, Metalogic and Neutrality." *Erkenntnis* 79:211–231.

Wright, Crispin. 1992. *Truth and Objectivity*. Harvard University Press.

2013. "A Plurality of Pluralisms." In Nikolaj Jang Lee Linding Pedersen and Cory D. Wright (eds.), *Truth and Pluralism: Current Debates*, 123–153. Oxford University Press.

Wyatt, Nicole. 2004. "What Are Beall and Restall Pluralists About?" *Australasian Journal of Philosophy* 82:409–420.

Cambridge Elements=

# Philosophy and Logic

### Bradley Armour-Garb
*SUNY Albany*

Bradley Armour-Garb is chair and Professor of Philosophy at SUNY Albany. His books include *The Law of Non-Contradiction* (co-edited with Graham Priest and J. C. Beall, 2004), *Deflationary Truth and Deflationism and Paradox* (both co-edited with J. C. Beall, 2005), *Pretense and Pathology* (with James Woodbridge, Cambridge University Press, 2015), *Reflections on the Liar* (2017), and *Fictionalism in Philosophy* (co-edited with Fred Kroon, 2020).

### Frederick Kroon
*The University of Auckland*

Frederick Kroon is Emeritus Professor of Philosophy at the University of Auckland. He has authored numerous papers in formal and philosophical logic, ethics, philosophy of language, and metaphysics, and is the author of *A Critical Introduction to Fictionalism* (with Stuart Brock and Jonathan McKeown-Green, 2018).

### About the Series

This Cambridge Elements series provides an extensive overview of the many and varied connections between philosophy and logic. Distinguished authors provide an up-to-date summary of the results of current research in their fields and give their own take on what they believe are the most significant debates influencing research, drawing original conclusions.

# Cambridge Elements

# Philosophy and Logic

## Elements in the Series

*Temporal Logics*
Valentin Goranko

*The Many Faces of Impossibility*
Koji Tanaka and Alexander Sandgren

*Relevance Logic*
Shay Allen Logan

*Propositional Quantifiers*
Peter Fritz

*Logic and Information*
Edwin Mares

*The Logic of Grounding*
Fabrice Correia

*Meinongianism*
Maria Elisabeth Reicher

*Free Logic: A Generalization*
Greg Frost-Arnold

*Probability and Inductive Logic*
Antony-Eagle

*Logic and Science: An Exploration of Logical Anti-Exceptionalism*
Filippo Ferrari and Massimiliano Carrara

*Nonmonotonic Logic*
Christian Straßer

*Logical Pluralism*
Colin R. Caret

A full series listing is available at: www.cambridge.org/EPL

For EU product safety concerns, contact us at Calle de José Abascal, 56–1°, 28003 Madrid, Spain or eugpsr@cambridge.org.

www.ingramcontent.com/pod-product-compliance
Lightning Source LLC
LaVergne TN
LVHW020350260326
834688LV00045B/1639